Streams of
Consciousness

ALSO BY THE AUTHOR:

Pale Morning Done

Streams of
Consciousness
≈ Hip-Deep Dispatches from the River of Life

JEFF HULL

THE LYONS PRESS
Guilford, Connecticut
An imprint of The Globe Pequot Press

To buy books in quantity for corporate use
or incentives, call **(800) 962–0973, ext. 4551,**
or e-mail **premiums@GlobePequot.com.**

The Lyons Press is an imprint of The Globe Pequot Press.

10 9 8 7 6 5 4 3 2 1
Printed in the United States of America

ISBN-13: 978- 1-59228-988-2
ISBN-10: 1-59228-988-6

Library of Congress Cataloging-in-Publication Data is available on file.

Some of the essays in this collection have been published in different forms
in the following magazines: Fly Rod & Reel— "Chasing Grayling,"
"Schoolies in Session," "Brothers in Waiting," "Bitterroot River," "Rorshach
Bluegill," and "Zorro"; Adventure West magazine—"Slough Creek";
Private Club— "Grand Slam"; Fly Fisherman— "Third Spaces."

Contents

Off the Land   3

Chasing Grayling   13

Schoolies in Session   23

Blackfeet Lake Tales   37

Brothers in Waiting   49

Blue Moon, Blue Sharks   53

Slough Creek   67

Bitterroot River   77

Keepers   85

Rorschach Bluegill   99

The Grand Slam   111

Third Spaces   123

Knots   143

Estancia del Zorro   155

Saint Juice   165

Wonder Time   187

Streams of
Consciousness

Off the Land

WE FOUND A SPOT, a slow pool in an elbow of a brush-choked feeder creek. It would be tempting to romanticize here, to remember this place as a lovely pool of stream in a cathedral-like sylvan glade, but the truth is there was not much lovely about it. In our corner of northwest Ohio, the rivers and creeks ran torpid with mud, silted and fudgey. This creek was only slightly clearer, the color of tea with a touch of cream. The woods were ragged and overgrown, a carnival of weeds, and the ground held a bouncy layer of rotting leaves. Our spot was not far from County Road 17, only a short way through the woods. People on the road could probably glimpse the colors of our clothing in gaps through the trees, if they looked. The high school athletic director's house was only a few hundred yards away.

At our spot, the creek took a bend to the left. Deadwood had fallen and backed flat, muddy water above it in the bend. Brush crowded the banks, and tree trunks stood behind the brush and exploded overhead, a continuous unraveling of leaves that lent each day the feel of twilight. It was difficult to cast, but we didn't really need to cast. We called this place the Combat Zone—because we wanted to see the world as exciting and action packed we tended to cast most situations in dramatic us-against-the-world terms—and in early March of our junior year in high school, the white bass were stacked in that hole so thick you could ladle them out with a bucket. Instead we used spreaders and Garcia reels and Ugly Stik rods. We were proud of our Ugly Stiks. Johnny Bird and Digger Lytle and I would drive to the Combat Zone right from school, and by dark we could catch one hundred fifty white bass.

We were pretty simple midwestern boys, all the standard stuff. We wore sneakers everywhere and white tube socks with purple stripes—school colors—around the calf. I think maybe tube socks had just recently come out, although it could be that tube socks had been around a lot longer, and we hadn't noticed until we reached a certain age.

Digger drove a Buick Skylark, wrinkled with dents, and Johnny had a blue Chevy Nova with mags that he washed all the time. Digger and I both had blond hair, which we parted in the middle like John Denver and everybody else. We both stood tall and rangy, although Digger was taller, and when Digger stood in front of you his hips buckled forward slightly so his head seemed tilted far back and away, giving his demeanor some lazy confidence. Johnny Bird was shorter but stockier. He had hair that was stiff, the color and shape of a rusted wire brush.

We were not farm boys, but we were boys from a farm town—squirrel hunters and bullhead fishermen. We knew about the woods and the lake and the river and the nature of quarry and killing in the way you know things before you stop to think about them, the way you act and know things. But every time we fished in the Combat Zone we were astounded by the apparent endlessness of the fish. We could pull a hundred fish out of this pool—not much larger than the average above-ground backyard swimming pools that were starting to pop up in our town back then—come back the next day and take a hundred more. It was as if the bass sprung from an underground source, some endlessly surging spring.

For the white bass, this was their spawning run. The fish schooled in Lake Erie, then surged across the mudflats of Sandusky Bay, injected themselves upstream into the Sandusky River, and pulsed into the tiny feeder creeks to reproduce. For the bass, it was all about procreation. Females announced their readiness by swimming up to the surface. Several males rushed after one, and eggs and milt were released in a quick, impersonal gush. The eggs sank back down through the stream, their sticky coating adhering to the first solid object they came into contact with. This spawning was a prodigious event. One female white bass can produce over a million eggs a year (compared to two to five thousand for, say, rainbow trout). Nobody knows how many white bass are in the western basin of Lake Erie, but there were never any limits on how many fish we could keep.

In the shadow-dappled light of the woods, deep beneath the surface of the water, the fish we hooked flashed frantically, flipping and twisting. I remember watching Johnny hooking a fish, watching the bass flashing in the water, its light traceable like the path of a sparkler in the night. And when Johnny pulled the fish from the creek, twirling from the blue monofilament thread that connected it to the bowed rod tip, the fish clamped its jaws firmly shut and pinched out long, last streams of semen.

Johnny was disappointed when that happened because he and Digger usually fished side by side on a mud spit and Johnny liked to milk fish semen onto Digger's leg when he had the chance. Digger got even in different ways. We insulted each other constantly and laughed it off because it was the time in our lives when we first began to suspect that self-doubt was something we were going to have to live with and was perhaps a part of everybody's life.

In April and May of our junior year, this fishing was about goofing off, surely, but not so much as it was about booze. Booze and sex—we had stumbled across the connections. We were kids who worked during the summer vacation, mowing weeds or digging ditches or driving delivery trucks so we could amass cash for car payments and car insurance payments and gas and a cache of spending money designed to last throughout the school year, which, by spring, had always run out.

So we caught fish, white bass from the Combat Zone, and we sold them. We sold them so that we could buy booze, which could lead to sex in some form, because that was the driving interest of our lives. We all had felt sex at least once and were committed to it. Digger Lytle, according to him, had already been with several girls. Johnny and I had long-standing girlfriends with whom we had finally had sex. Mine was a brown-haired girl with smiles that told you even she thought she was silly.

On Fridays she and I drove, silently, under the last stoplight in town and on into the country night. Lights fell away from the roadside until only pinpoints in the distance marked the broad darkness. We rode down a county two lane, through flat fields in the night, smelling the musk of spring beans and cabbage pushing up through the mocha soil. I took her to a forgotten covered bridge over a trickling creek in the middle of nowhere. The covered bridge was no longer open to traffic, but a rutted lane led from the county road to it. The lane was lined on both sides by tall weeping willows, their new leaves bright in the night, as if lit from within.

We parked on the graveled widening of the lane where it ended at the bridge and, without talking about it much, climbed into the backseat. Now and then headlights from the county road would pierce the dark like paper cones. She always clenched her teeth until the lights passed. We made love, and every time we did I wanted immediately—even if my body wasn't ready—to do it again. What we had then were pure moments, not only because we were in love, but because we were young bodies learning by feel.

We should have left it at that, but we didn't. In the way that always seems to happen, something else came along that made us think we wanted something different. We were so young—I was sixteen; she was a year younger—that all of our decisions remained riddled with that pervasive self-doubt. It would be years before we even knew what the word "inhibition" meant, but we already felt that, when we drank a couple of beers or split a bottle of cheap wine, something different happened. We had not been drinking the first several months that we experimented with making love. But later we did drink, and the things we said and did to each other in the backseat headed toward reckless.

My girlfriend was a Catholic, and for her, I think, booze temporarily shushed the parents and priests and the things she'd been taught to believe. For me there was, or so it felt for that short, giddy period, less in the way. I wanted booze to drown the self-consciousness, and my friends wanted booze for the same reasons, and for booze we needed money. So when the sun set and bats twirled crazily over the twilit pool and it was too dark to fish in the Combat Zone any longer, Johnny and Digger and I took our stringers and buckets packed full of white bass, fish frozen in stiff, dead curves, and we drove to the Sand Docks.

The Sand Docks were low gravel banks along the Sandusky River on the downstream edge of town, below an abandoned water treatment plant. They were unofficial garbage dumps. Refuse littered the banks. Rats flitted between brush piles. Compost rotted underfoot. In the spring, the Sand Docks were crowded with dented and rusted El Caminos and low-slung Eldorados and cars not terribly unlike the ones we rode around in, only longer and lower to the ground.

The Sand Docks were flat, oil-grimed gravel, and the banks were almost level with the river rushing by. People sat on upside-down five-gallon buckets at the river's edge, fishing. Almost to a man the fishermen on the sand docks were black. They drove down from Toledo and Detroit to fish the great white bass run on the Sandusky River.

We parked along the Sand Docks after dark and wandered among these men, hands in our pockets, trying not to appear smug or vulnerable. We walked among the small camps the fishermen divided themselves into, fires, cars—the Sand Dock fishermen often slept in their cars—or drag-along campers, and we found the fishermen who seemed to not be doing so well. We looked for heaps of fresh empties, or the longer glints from empty whiskey bottles in the dark. These belonged to the men who could tell their wives they were going away to fish, but mostly went because it was the act of going somewhere else, and they drank.

We found a bleary man in the dark sprawled out in the backseat of his car with the door open; or leaning against a battered camper with green trim, an older man, older than he ought to be, with wet, red slivers in the sag of his lower eyelids and gray smoking the edges of his close-cropped hair.

"Want some fish?" Digger asked.

"Whachou got?" the man would say. He wore a gray hooded sweatshirt with the sleeves ripped off, work pants cured with motor oil, a plaid shirt, and a cap.

"We got fish."

"Where they at? I don't see no fish."

We motioned for him to follow, walked him back to our car. Digger opened the trunk and Johnny and I held up fish, stringers like long bunches of bananas, only slimy and silver in the night. More fish—heaped in buckets, piled on newspapers—glistened in the trunk.

"How much you want?" the man asked.

"Want 'em all?"

"I don't know if I want 'em all, now."

"How many you want?" Digger asked. Digger always did the bargaining. He liked it, and, to be honest, Johnny and I were a little afraid.

"How many you got there? How many is that?" the man asked, peering into the trunk, his head bobbing to see all the fish.

The first time, Digger said, "We'll give you twenty-five for ten bucks."

"Deal!" the man said, and before we even realized we had undersold, he pressed a ten spot in Digger's hand.

In later transactions Digger would be more savvy. "Twenty-five fish for twenty bucks," he'd start with. This was too much. Fifteen, we learned, was the price point the market would bear. But Digger would say twenty, just to see if there was any movement. At this point the man we were selling to usually produced from somewhere in his clothing a small bottle. It was MD 20/20. Or Boone's Farm. Or a flat pint of Wild Turkey. He offered it to us, Digger first, who gave it to Johnny, who passed it to me. The gesture was sincere. The black men at the Sand Docks treated us like adults.

"How much for forty?" the man would ask.

"Ain't selling forty," Digger said.

"I don't want no fifty."

"We'll give you twenty for fifteen," Digger said, and the dealing was done, their paper bills exchanged for our stiff fish. We could drift back onto the Sand Docks, searching for other men, more cash for the rest of our white bass.

We could have told them; they asked where we got all the fish. We could have said, "Follow us," and led them in our car the few miles to the creek, showed them where to park beside the culvert, pointed out the path through the woods to the bend in the water and the deep pool of the Combat Zone. I think now of what a spectacle that would have been, letting those men haul white bass from our spot, letting them see the flashing in the muddy water, feel the tug and jerk on the rod in their shaky drinkers' hands, letting them watch the milt running opalescent over their fingers and the expelled eggs tacky on the skin of their palms as they handled fish. We could have let them fill buckets and stringers with their catch—it was not much harder work than the heavy drinking they toiled over at the Sand Docks.

But *we* had found the place, and we wanted to be the ones astonished by the sheer numbers of fish in the creek bend. It made us think we had something to do with the stream and the fish and those extraordinary catches, that our powers of discovery had led to this bonanza, rather than the other way around. Of course our expression of gratitude for being granted this amazement was to nearly wipe out an entire spawning population. We weren't the clearest thinkers, which was apparent even in the name we gave the place. We had already bought into a certain American myth about fishing and hunting. It was us against them. We tended to imagine ourselves doing battle against wily adversaries, as if the fish knew we were up there on the bank and were deploying every evasive tactic they knew to outfox us. This plagues the literature and remains the great failing of outdoorsmen even today.

Those fish were just spawning, that's all. Abundance of this nature grows so rare in the world, the great aggregations and movements of animals that used to mark the seasons on the land. We have the great salmon runs, but the salmon are dying, nearly all of them in steep decline and no political will to save them. We have amazing sardine runs on the coasts, but we are not taking care of the coasts in any way that can sustain those runs. We have caribou, though oil hunger threatens those migrations. Hundreds of thousands of snow geese still fly up the Rocky Mountain Front, and uncountable waterfowl still gather on northern lakes in the boreal forest. But it grows increasingly more difficult to find these spectacles of mutual intent.

We could have made anything we wanted of that abundance at the Combat Zone. We chose to make money with it. True, our underlying motivations were not so different from those that drew the bass across the mudflats and into creeks, into that elbow where their lives happened to intersect with ours, and end. But the difference is this: those fish were responding to ancient rhythms, whereas in the human imagination, any time can be springtime. The motions of the natural world reveal a simplicity of intent that the human imagination consistently betrays to suit the ideas we have built around ourselves, to get what we think it is we should want. And even that seems always changing.

It's been twenty-five years since I last saw the Combat Zone. It's possible that white bass teem in that pool unmolested, more fish than ever. I don't honestly know. It occurs to me that I never knew much about that creek, or the fish we found there, except in terms of what I could take from it. We never really tried to know it, any more than we ever talked to the men on the Sand Docks about anything other than money and dead fish. We took. Knowing is what we missed. We gave nothing to the story of those places. If I'm lucky, it's not too late to start.

Chasing Grayling

THE DENSE FIRS ALONG the road stand darker than the evening sky. A bat skitters around the tip of my fly rod, an ellipse gone out of control. Directly overhead the coming dark is as soft as butter. Dusk in the Big Hole is the land returning to itself, and it's easy to see that we're not what it's here for.

Joel is leaning on his elbows against the side of the pickup bed with a beer in his hand, and watching me take my waders off. Joel is a poet. There are two kinds of poets: skinny poets and fat poets. Joel is a skinny poet, with a sharp face and edges of beard along his jaw. He looks like I imagine Vincent van Gogh would look on any average Tuesday: hungry, tense, brilliant, possibly mad. Tonight Joel looks slightly frustrated—he's new to fly fishing—and tired, but content to be both.

Content to be here, maybe, is the thing. We are standing along the northwestern shoulder of the Big Hole valley on a timbered bench that overlooks a small creek winding through pastureland. Willow clumps mark the watercourse. A few miles downstream the creek will meet another creek and become the Big Hole River, the home of the last population of fluvial grayling in the lower forty-eight. The reason we are here—I'm not sure Joel knows this—is to catch one of those bullet-shaped fish.

I go for the truck's door; the dome light opens something new and central in our small part of the night and Joel says, "I don't know about this women and trout stuff. I haven't caught that many trout, so I don't think I fully understand the metaphor."

There was nothing to it, idle talk, women and trout, but now I see a quick link and say, "When you first became attracted to women, did you catch many of them?"

Joel smiles. The world is that much more connected for him.

Or not.

After I skin the waders from my feet and slip into tennis shoes, after the first moments that I feel the night breeze on my sweaty legs and after the soft *whump* of the waders hitting the bed of the truck, I hear the creek behind me. It comes up from beneath the lowest branches of the trees. It is keeping everything moving.

Whatever happens between grayling and me, they are already part of my memory. When I fish for them, woven into the experience comes a moment of content in the Big Hole valley, standing beside the truck with Joel the poet. That moment won't wholly return, but it comes close, and it's one worth coming close to. Our world is about nothing more than coalesced memory, sharing everybody's moments.

That night at the Big Hole, Joel and I drank from a fifth of Johnny Walker and threw sage on the fire for scent. We talked about our families, trying to tell each other where we had come from, what had brought us to this. Much later we drank more and proceeded to indulge in philosophy. Joel was so moved as to throw up all over the countryside, and we both passed out atop our small hillock. But for a while there, before the whiskey took over—even while the whiskey was warm but before it was blinding—we had something. A real attempt at communion, at any rate, and those are too few, too far between in a lifetime.

As are grayling in Montana. But before they are gone, grayling can give me a peek at that crafty bastard History. Grayling in the Big Hole are glacial remnants, a population of animals left behind by the ice ages of lore. I don't know that there even were ice ages, but History tells me that there were and that grayling should be proof. Biologists who study the history of species say that Montana grayling were once the genetic compatriots of the Arctic genus, that grayling ranged from the waters of Alaska, the Yukon, and the Northwest Territories down through British Columbia and Alberta, into Montana.

The biologists say Montana grayling were isolated by retreating glaciers; still, they thrived for centuries. The fish were once found in all the tributaries of the Missouri River above Great Falls: the Madison, Jefferson, Beaverhead, Ruby, Gallatin, Big Hole, Sun, Smith, and Teton rivers. But grayling do not adapt well. Once white civilization festooned the valleys of western Montana, grayling didn't last long.

We did nothing to take care of them, and by and large we still don't. In 1983, Montana Fish, Wildlife, and Parks biologist Dick Oswald counted 111 adult grayling per stream mile in the Big Hole. In 1989 Pat Byorth counted 27 per mile. Current estimates indicate a weak stabilization around 34 fish per mile. After many years of negotiations and threatened lawsuits, conservationists and ranchers reached an agreement to maintain a certain amount of water in the Big Hole River, even during irrigating season—enough water to keep the river cool and provide cover so that grayling could survive. It would be a great first step, this agreement, except certain ranchers with senior water rights routinely ignore it and take as much water as they want. At times during June and July, the Big Hole is bled to less than twenty cubic feet per second—not much bigger than your average street gutter after a brisk rain. Stretches of the river come close to disappearing altogether.

Outside the Big Hole, grayling have vanished. Glacial remnants, the argument goes. Relicts. Would have been gone anyway. This is what we tell ourselves when we want to log a new hillside, graze cattle on a spawning stream, or build a new trophy home.

I caught my first grayling two years after my initial trip to the Big Hole. By chance, Joel was with me again, and we were driving through the lower end of the immense flat that is the upper Big Hole valley. The road had begun to lift and bank slightly as the land rolled into hills in preparation for racing down the canyon to come. But at that point, the river—just downstream from Fishtrap Creek—was still calm, broad, and shallow, casually rolling through the ranchland and sage.

The water was stained by tannic acid, a reddish pigment that leaches into the stream from adjacent bogs and marshes and turns the slow-moving water the color of sun tea. This was likely Joel's last trip to the Big Hole for some time, one of the last trips we would take together. He was off to Japan to live and, he hoped, to teach. That's what poets do best—live and teach.

Joel and I stopped where two braids of water sluiced together over a shallow gravel bed to form a fairly fast riffle. The riffle tilted into a broad-based pool, broken into feeding lanes by cow-sized boulders. Flecks of foam marked the tailing and merging of currents. I waded across the pool at the base of the riffle, found the water waist-deep, warmer than I would have liked, and reddened by tannins. I heard the flip of a fish feeding in the riffle near the far bank. I cast at a foam line. Not pleased with my placement, I lifted my fly from the water and cast again, then a third time.

Then I liked where my fly landed and I let it ride the riffle until the foam began. I turned momentarily to watch Joel loose his line and cast into the near side of the pool, and in that moment something happened, not a movement I sighted or a break in the tinkling of the riffle, but something was different suddenly and I knew my fly had been struck. I lifted my rod and heard the rip of line coming off the water announcing that a live weight held down the other end. The line stretched against my hand and began to surge, bouncing the rod tip.

The fish furrowed under the riffle, holding tight against the current. Then it let go, swept swiftly back with the water's flow, and began twisting and jerking. As it swam in choppy, darted arcs around me, I could see the flash of its body in the reddish water, and I knew it was not a trout. The fish writhed and jerked its chin all the way in, but it was small and I brought it to hand quickly to save its strength.

In the net I saw my first grayling. I have heard grayling compared to mountain whitefish (a close relative). Unlike trout, whitefish have large scales. Grayling, too, are coated with evenly lined rows of scales. For me the likeness ends there.

Where a whitefish is copper, grayling are pewter. A grayling's mouth is small but is not turned to the bottom of its face like that of the bottom-feeding whitefish. In the essence of grayling I see less whitefish, more bonefish. The shapes are similar, ballistic. In both bonefish and grayling, beauty is iridescent. Grayling sheen roseate and lavender. Color on their flanks operates with the shifting waver of the aurora borealis—never predictable, never fixed. And then there is the dorsal, unique to these fish, an opaque sail spotted with purple and teal, used for display in territorial disputes.

I cupped the fish, a twelve-incher, in the crooks of my fingers and submerged it in the water, cradling it by the tail and under the fins and rocking it back and forth to work oxygen through its gills. For a while, the little grayling did not move against me; it let me ease its body back and forth. Then I felt the fish twitch, flex. I opened my hand slowly. The grayling hovered for a moment before shimmying away, angled upstream and deep.

Joel caught one next, and I caught another and Joel caught his second. Grayling are social animals. They congregate near their own. Their social structures are acutely realized—preordained, actually—with larger fish occupying the upstream end of the pool and the others filling in behind according to size. Two fish interested in the same territory line up beside each other and flare dorsal fins.

That's the contest. The bigger fish wins and the smaller drops downstream. A grayling may stay in the same pool, a few inches from a minute rock pattern in the streambed, for an entire summer. They will migrate sometimes sixty miles to rearrange themselves in winter holes. Joel and I could have stayed and caught grayling all day, maybe caught all the fish in the pool, but that was not our aim.

It took us twenty minutes to catch two each, and almost all of that was release time. That Joel and I took the extra few minutes to see that the fish we caught regained their equilibrium before sending them back into the stream was a rare treat for the grayling. With few exceptions, people have done almost nothing to see that grayling remain healthy and swim strongly.

Instead we have sucked water from streams for irrigation, removing microhabitat and food sources and raising water temperatures. We have allowed cows to trample riparian zones where aquatic insects reproduce. We've stripped the hillsides of trees, cutting away natural defenses against erosion and allowing silt to pile into the water, silently clogging the streambeds and, again, erasing microhabitat so crucial to young-of-the-year fish trying to avoid predation.

We have introduced exotic species—rainbow, brown, and brook trout—which consistently outcompete grayling for habitat and food. We've gone about our business and, in a manner that is as American as you can get, have paid absolutely no attention to what our business is doing to the world around us. The grayling responded by dying off.

⌘

After Joel and I caught our first two grayling, we fished on upstream. In another pool we caught some small brook trout, and in the mud along the stream bank we found the fresh print of a black bear.

When we worked our way back, we saw a young man fishing in the grayling pool. He stood on one of the boulders and cast badly. We walked back along the banks, stood one hundred yards away at the truck, and watched as he ripped back on his rod, setting the hook. He horsed the fish in and we could see the mercury sheen; knew it was a grayling. The young man had no net. He lifted his rod, and the grayling, flapping wildly to escape, smacked itself over and over against the rock. When the young man finally grabbed the fish, he tore the hook from its mouth and tossed the grayling underhand into the air. We watched as the grayling slammed against the water and, stunned, floated downstream to die.

Just as quickly the young man caught another fish and repeated the scene. I wanted to go down and kick him in the ass, kick him right into the river. Joel and I decided to leave right then, before I did something we would regret. As we drove away, a camper pulled up and I could see the boy raise his fist to the man driving the camper—his father, I guessed. Rolling down the Big Hole valley toward the narrows of the canyon, I felt uneasy and still furious, because this boy had ruined my beautiful moment, my first grayling.

I cared, that much I felt righteous about, but caring was all I had done, and the farther I drove the more uneasy I became knowing that. Taking my little moment and running was what I was really up to. Trying to hoard the memory so that I could polish it up later, buff out the part about the kid and the dead fish.

About ten miles down the road, Joel the poet scratched his scraggly beard and said, "You know, I bet that kid didn't even know how to release a fish. That's what we should have done. We should have just said, 'Excuse me, I don't mean to be an asshole, but can I just show you something . . .?'"

I wish I could say we went back, but we didn't. We swished our venom around in our mouths, spit a little on each other, and had another beer, disgusted with ourselves. Joel was right. There are ways to act. There are ways to share with people what you've learned about how to act. Maybe next time I'll catch on quicker. Maybe even in time to do something.

Schoolies in Session

WE WERE PUSHING THE season. That's what Steven Dodd told us. This was the second week in May. The striped bass were maybe around, maybe not, but they weren't in all their usual haunts yet, Dodd said. Tough to find.

This was specifically *not* what he had told me back in February, when ice locked up the rivers of western Montana, where I live, and cold wind blasted gray surf along the coastline of southeastern Connecticut, where he lives. Back in February, when my friend Dan Bennett and I were driven by the grinding Montana winter to consider desperate gestures like ice fishing and nymphing in an anxious compunction to get ourselves into some new fish, Dodd thought the second week in May would be fine. In fact, he had made the classic blunder of spouting, "Second week in May? Oh, I guarantee we'll get you into some stripers."

It should be pointed out (although it should also become obvious) that Dodd is not, by any stretch of the imagination, a fishing guide. He's a businessman and an old friend. But he and his brothers and uncles and cousins have been fishing the coastal waters around the Rhode Island-Connecticut border since they were kids. Then, Dodd was just fishing. Now he's a bit whacked out about it. "OK, so maybe I'm addicted," Dodd says. "So what? It's not like I'm hurting anybody with my problem."

Dodd keeps notebooks jammed full of records of every fish he catches and what the tide was doing when he caught it and where the wind was from and how fast it was blowing and what color lure he used and how he retrieved it and what the water temperature was, and so, although I believe this all to be a bit fervid, I trusted him about the stripers. I met Dodd when I lived in Rhode Island and he was my next-door neighbor. Then I found out he was into fishing too. By and by that led to chasing schoolies, stripers in the three- to six-pound range. These were not the raging bulls that would sweep up the coast later in the summer, but a six-pound bass on a 6-weight rod sounded like plenty of fun for me.

Dodd doesn't know much about fly fishing. He's into ultra-light spinning gear. There are arguments that go around and around about that, which I won't get into because all I wanted to say is that Dodd was quite proud of the fact that he had the compunction to line us up with a guy who ran a yuppie fly shop just across the border in Rhode Island, who, we would learn with experience, didn't know much about fly fishing either. At least not for stripers.

At least not when you're pushing the season. After selling me seventy dollars' worth of saltwater flies—OK, I didn't know much about fly fishing for stripers, either—the fly-shop guy directed us to Quonochontaug Pond—which, I think I should mention, is hardly a secret. In Montana that would be advice on the level of telling somebody that the hot spot to fish would be, say, the Bighorn. Or the Yellowstone. But the next day, when we had determined time and tide to be most advantageous, we got ourselves to the Quonnie pond. We arrived just before sunset after driving a narrow road down a point of spring-green land. To our left a boat channel cut the beach grass. Before us and to our right stretched the salt pond. Channel markers ran out into it about a hundred and fifty yards before jagging to the right, on inland.

Footprints of small children and raccoon and a scrim of gull prints marked the sandy mud at the water's edge. The short, green grass dropped on a carved coastline, an eroded lip along the water, marking high tide. Terns intermittently splashed into the water in the rip beyond the channel marker. We waded across seventy-five yards of shallow flat that filled the pond between the boat channel and the point. The water, crystal clear, ran only a few inches deep until the edge of the channel, which was marked exactly by a line of crushed white shell.

Dodd stepped down waist-deep into the channel cut and cast his spinning rod, silhouetted by a huge orange sun. Current welled and mushroomed behind his waist, and beyond him depth, wind, and tide riffled and ripped the water into blue brushwork blocks, each seeming to move in opposing directions. I stepped down the steep edge of the channel and began to work my fly, a white sand eel imitation. Dodd had been on the phone with fishing buddies all week and had learned that what erratic catching had been going on had been done on smallish flies. The water was warming, reaching the fifty-degree mark, and an alewives run had begun, but the bass seemed to be feeding on thin, yellow-sided minnows, locally known as spearing, and on sand eels.

The whistle of our flies and the whoosh of Dodd's lure being cast filled the air, and I felt the suck of tide eroding sand from around my feet. When water filled the flat, stripers would wait just off the edge of the channel for bait to be swept off the flats into the drop. Behind us, a hundred yards away on shore, because the water carried their voices, we heard someone say, "What are they after? Bonefish?" Then the sun went down and the sky and water darkened and phosphorescence began to fill the current's wake behind me. It showered in front of me when I moved up the channel as if I were kicking green embers from a fire. Serious bass fishermen won't fish when there's too much phosphorescence because the bass—particularly bigger, older bass—can spot flashes from a monofilament line.

The night deepened and I could see my fly line rip a streak of green sparks from the dark water as I lifted it to back cast. My arm stiffened from so much casting and I spent long spells standing and watching the lights from shore work in long silver slivers on the surface of the flats. Dan, who had never fished for stripers, didn't know whether the long fishless pace was something he should expect in this new endeavor, and so he pretended to look around and understand exactly what was happening. At eleven thirty we quit. Dodd said he had felt one solid strike, but what else was he going to say? We waded back across the flats, our thighs pushing ripples with the tide across the still water, glimmering in the shore lights.

We hit Quonochontaug the next night, arriving later in the tide and staying later. Nothing. "This is going to be a great spot in another couple of weeks," Dodd said. Dan and I assured him we found that fascinating.

Late the next night we drove over to the Thames River at Groton where Dodd's uncle had told him we could expect to get into fish. Everybody we talked to had a pointer about where we could "get into fish." Dodd stopped at all the tackle shops where the proprietors each told us how to get into fish. In the parking lot outside Dodd's office, a man spotted our fly rods and stopped to offer tips about where to get into fish. Dodd's business associates all knew how to get into fish.

But Uncle Dick was a different character, a crafty, cunning old salt, a fellow who wouldn't fish his hot spots in the daylight for fear that somebody else might find them. At night he doused his lights when he approached his holes or if he suspected someone was following him. He always rigged his rods with his hands below the gunnel lest someone with binoculars spotted his lure combos. Dodd had imbued Uncle Dick with legendary features, including a sort of charming disrespect for rules that kept him on close, personal terms with the local game-law enforcement officials. But he left no doubt that Uncle Dick always knew where the bass were.

There was some question about whether Uncle Dick would take us out with him. He had his secrets to keep. Over the phone he told Dodd about the spot on the Thames we tried. Again, we were blanked and nobody spotted a fish. "Dick brought me here once before and we caught bass all along these pilings," Dodd said, pointing his rod tip at wood posts slanted in the dark, remnants from a logging operation. "It's just too early in the season."

The fourth day Dan and I decided to hell with this striper chasing, we were going trout fishing. We headed to the Farmington River, arriving in time to catch the tail end of a prolific Hendrickson hatch. But temperatures climbed into the nineties—the first truly hot day of the year—and the sudden differential kicked up blasting winds that made casting erratic at best and dusted the bugs right off the water. Dan and I hooked a few nice trout between gusts, but within the hour the wind grew steady and it became obvious that we were done. On the drive home Dodd told honeymoon stories about standing on a salt flat in Belize, bonefishing, when the guide, who remained aboard the skiff, was so intent on finding bones that he didn't notice how Dodd and his newly wedded wife—who stood in thigh-deep water—were spending all their time doinking small blacktip reef sharks on the nose with the end of the rods so that the sharks, attracted by the smell of shrimp they had been using for bait, didn't pop the balls of their calves off or clip their Achilles tendons.

We rose at five thirty the following morning and motored Dodd's fifteen-foot fiberglass dory up the Pawcatuck River, for reasons nobody could quite explain. Actually I believe we did that because the yuppie fly-shop guy told us that right at high tide the bass would be up the river mouth, feeding like packs of wild dogs. We puttered around the Pawcatuck casting at bassy-looking banks and rock piles, pilings, and small cove mouths. At each spot Dodd would describe in enthusiastic detail just how fishy the place looked, or how later in the season this place was going to be hopping.

"You're a week too early," he would say, and shake his head sadly, as if he could have told us so. By the end of the morning, he had reduced himself to muttering, and Dan and

I had reduced ourselves to not trying to listen. We caught nothing. We saw nothing, except that I spotted a crack in the ferrule of the 8-weight Winston rod I was using to buck the wind. It was a borrowed rod.

At this point the trip was looking sort of shot through the hips. Dodd got desperate and resorted to unsportsmanlike conduct. He called his Uncle Dick. "I'll pay him to play it clean if I have to," Dodd said, "but you guys have to go out with this guy. He will, I promise you, get you into fish."

When Dodd called, Uncle Dick said maybe, maybe not he would take us out. Had to see. But we should try this spot along the Thames. Dodd said we tried the spot he had told us. "Oh not that spot," Uncle Dick said, "the bass aren't there." He told us a different spot. "Get there on the ebbing tide," he said.

At the second spot, to Uncle Dick's credit, we could see swirls off the bank and the splash of bait leaping from the water of the wide river, perhaps sixty yards out in the current. Far, far beyond my casting range and Dan's. On our side the river dropped immediately to a depth beyond wading. We walked down the bank, following the apparent movement of the schools, heading downriver with the tide. The swirls were, by this point, lovely rosettes of affirmation, beautiful in the relief they brought. Dodd kept saying wait, they work in big loops. They'll circle toward the bank. But they didn't and this was maddening.

"I tell you," Dodd said, "in a week or two I'd know exactly where to find them up against the bank."

Driving away from the river we saw something interesting: somebody had lost an axle on a boat trailer and had rolled both the trailer and the aluminum johnboat over the guardrail of the road. "Poor bastard," Dodd said. Then, "Hey, wait a minute."

There was silver-haired Uncle Dick, built like an old grappler in a green T-shirt, hurling and kicking pieces of debris off the road. He had been driving over to see if we had taken him up on his advice, and he had brought his boat, which, I probably don't need to point out, could have carried us to within easy casting range of the feeding striper schoolies. But his boat was piled over the guardrail, engine and trolling motor demolished. When the cop came—a short, potbellied man with an incredible last name chock-full of consonants—he looked us over.

"Fishing?" he asked.

"Trying to," Dodd said.

"You try just up from the railroad bridge? Ought to be able to get into some fish there."

Then the cop tried to trap us into admitting that we had been drinking beer.

Dan and I decided that the best possible thing to do next would be to go to Maine. Dan had never been to Maine, and I held fond memories. Mainly, we needed a change, something to mix up the luck, which all seemed to be settled at the bottom of our jugs. "Find the fish," we told Dodd, "we'll be back in a couple of days."

The next morning we drove north, stopping to try a line in the Wood River in Rhode Island where deer flies assailed us in unmerciful and mean-spirited waves as soon as we stepped from the car. I had fever chills from the sheer number of bites while trying to rig up, and concurrently I noticed that I could not find the reel that went with my 6-weight rod, which I had been using since the 8-weight cracked.

We drove to Boothbay Harbor to have a late lunch of lobster and margaritas. The sun broke through the steel gray of

Maine clouds and warmed the wharf, and the seagulls stayed away. I've always felt that you're not eating lobster right unless you need a shower afterward, and we went at it with heartfelt butter and sloppy abandon. The next day we crossed New Hampshire into Vermont and fished the Battenkill for small trout, trading turns on Dan's rod. We found the fish flipping up for mayflies beneath a red covered bridge and took each one we cast to, beautiful brookies with rich white-fin edges and small butter-bellied browns with electric red spots. The world was better and that evening we drove back to Connecticut where I found my fly reel underneath a bed in Dodd's house. The tides for the next day appeared favorable, ebb beginning just at sunrise, and the wind was light from the south. On top of it all Dodd had gone out the night before and caught four bass.

We went to bed early, slept hard, and rose before dawn to find that we had lost the seventy dollars' worth of saltwater flies we had bought at the yuppie fly shop. Dan and I tore up the house and cars looking for the flies, but they were nowhere. For a moment I thought our fishing was done. I thought there was some sort of vicious destiny at work—because I was sure this was the morning we would get into fish—and I grew angry to the point that I was moments away from saying to hell with it and going back to bed. Dodd came jogging up from loading the boat to see what was keeping us. Then he said, "It's getting late. I'm usually headed back in by now."

Which made me wonder why he hadn't woke us earlier and did nothing to lighten the atmosphere. Nobody talked for a long moment. Then Dodd said, "Come on, you can use one of the things I use for droppers. Let's just go." It was apparent by the tone of his voice that he had given up too.

Anyway we headed out of the Lords Point cove into Fishers Island Sound, chugging along in Dodd's dory. We hugged close to the rocky shoreline, then rounding into Stonington Harbor. Dodd cut inside the breakwall and then we motored toward the Pawcatuck inlet, slipping just inside the western edge of Sandy Point—a long, low island only a few dozen yards across, just beach held together in the middle by a low line of beach grass, beach plums, and Rugosa rose. Sandy Point was once part of Napatree Point, which juts southeast into the sound from Watch Hill, Rhode Island, but the 1938 hurricane sheared Sandy Point off and, although it is still considered Rhode Island territory, the island has been on the march westward ever since. It now sits firmly in Connecticut water.

The uninhabited island is a huge gull rookery, but also the nesting grounds for a number of threatened birds, including piping plovers and roseate terns. As we cut inside the point, Dodd pointed out an oystercatcher standing on the edge of the water, a white-breasted bird with a black back and cap and a white swirl not unlike a killer whale's chinstrap on its shoulder, and a long, thin red bill for prying through the sand. Dodd seemed glad to see it.

Inside Sandy Point, the sun was just up and the early morning water offered a vista of flat, vaporous blue. Dodd cut the engine and stood to scan with his binoculars. The wake rolled away from behind the dory, leaving an aisle of bubbles where we crossed the still water. The river inlet was full of bait, and the air full of terns. The terns folded their thin wings and dropped, shattering the calm blue, but by the time they lifted into the air again, they left the surface whole behind them. Dodd scanned for rings on the water not made by terns. "People blow by schoolies in here all the time," he said, "because they're looking for something more obvious. Schoolies only leave small swirls, but they're right here."

Dodd spotted bass and moved us tight against Sandy Point. There was no great concentration of terns, but every direction I looked a bird or two hit the water. Spotty fish swirls bloomed on the still surface. Dodd gave me a fly with a lime epoxy body and tail streaked with a strip of Flashabou. He didn't know the name of it and neither do I, but when I placed a cast next to a swirl and started stripping, I saw beneath the surface a metallic green slash as a striper slammed the fly. Startled by the force of the take, I struck back hard.

The bass came right out of the water and flipped over. Then he ran deep and had his way with my 6-weight rod for a few minutes before I could bring him to the boat. The low angle of the sun sparkled the parallel green stripes along his head like sequins. It was not a big bass, three pounds perhaps, but the moment I held its weight on my palm, my evil mood—which had already begun to evaporate with the morning haze and the lilting water—vanished entirely.

The swirls stopped then, disappeared completely, so Dodd moved us around the eastern tip of Sandy Point, hunting for them. He found them in the middle of a frenzy. Huge schools of bait had washed out of the Pawcatuck around the end of Sandy Point, and the bass had trapped them in the shallows up against the outside corner. A constant chop marked the movement of the bait schools trying to avoid the pounding of the bass below. Cormorants and mergansers sat in the middle of the moil, diving regularly. A cloud of terns whirled and dropped into the water from overhead.

Dodd ran us up near the edge of the frenzy and shouted, "Get over."

"How deep is it?" I asked, the water so clear it could have been four or fourteen feet deep.

"Just get over!" Dodd shouted. Dan and I dropped over the gunnel, fully prepared to gush our waders full of chilly water. But I found bottom chest-deep and moved toward shore and the melee in front of me. The mergansers and cormorants flushed, flurrying across the water. Terns screamed high, gravelly screams, whirling everywhere, dropping and rising and dropping again. Bass boiled the water, bulging it before their shoulders as they plowed through the bait.

I cast into the garden of swirls and hooked up immediately. This fish was stronger than the first one and peeled line from me as the sweet reel music sang. The fish made muscular runs, a number of deep forays, while all around me the feeding frenzy raged on—bulges of water nearly hitting my chest, terns screaming, fluttering, splashing down—and I wanted to get this fish in so that I could hook another. I turned the bass into an arcing series of sideways sprints and finally corralled him against my hip. This striper went five or six pounds. I held him for a moment, sparkling in the sunlight, admiring how handsome a fish he was, then slipped him back into the sea.

Dan and I split, flanking the school and casting only a dozen or so yards in front of us. Almost immediately another solid strike stretched my line and I hit back. But I dropped my tip momentarily and the fish was gone. I remembered Dodd saying that you absolutely could not drop your tip once they were on because stripers are facile at turning their heads off a hook. I zapped the next fish.

I was fighting my fifth bass when it was over. I didn't notice until the striper was off and I looked up to start casting again and saw . . . nothing. No terns, no swirls, no bait, no bass shoulders, only the water moving smoothly under the sheen of the surface. As complete as the madness there was in its place silence and the sun was hot on my back and the salt water sticky on my hands and my arm was tired from casting and fighting.

But I was happy. Back on board the boat Dan's waders steamed from sweat and sun. We talked a little about setting the hook hard and quick. Dodd said that the shallows we were in were filled with eelgrass and that baitfish like to hide there. When the tide moves it tends to flatten the grass and strip the small fish of their cover. "They lose their trees," Dodd said.

Dodd had raked a popper across the school and caught a few himself. I suspected his pulse was still dancing like mine was. We talked and talked about catching the fish in such a frenzy, about fighting them. Dodd was talking about how good things would be in a few weeks. Dan and I made up a little song about what a hero Captain Dodd was. We were only coming up with things to say and do so that we didn't have to sit and stare at each other with big, goofy grins on our faces.

Then Dodd said, "You caught the first good day of the season."

"I thought we were pushing the season," I said.

"You pushed hard enough," Dodd said, but I bet he knew our pushing had little to do with it, that what paid off for us was just that strange mix of patience and impatience that keeps fishermen coming to the water.

Blackfeet Lake Tales

I STARED AT THE wind-whipped blue and green water of the small lake cupped between a low butte and the hips of the Rocky Mountain front. Beneath the lake's riffled surface I could almost feel the long, silent shapes ghosting over hidden ridges, shadowing dark drop-offs—the fabled trout of the Blackfeet Reservation. I can't fish the Blackfeet lakes without some visceral sensation of standing among spirits and ghosts. The broad, windswept landscape of the high plains and the jagged skyline of the Rocky Mountain cordillera, both bold and stark, undulate under the fluid roaming of lost and looming souls.

When Lewis and Clark came to this country the Blackfeet ruled the land and the land north of here to present-day Jasper, Alberta. Their dominion stretched south all the way down into the Yellowstone valley. The first of the Plains tribes to acquire guns, the Blackfeet were masters of whatever country they chose to travel. They are people who have historically been proud.

Now their sovereignty is limited in the United States to a wedge of high grasslands tucked along the border of Glacier National Park, a vacant range possessed by the swooping glide of low rolling hills and sudden gashing ravines, a land where unseen spirits seem as ever present as the scraps of fluttering trash pasted by wind against barbed wire fences. It is a distance marked by sudden breaks, and driving the dirt-sashed streets of towns called Browning, Babb, and Black-feet—tattered rural ghettos where new buildings look old and old buildings hold the town to the plains—it's easy to see that the breaks have not all been good ones.

This is a land also possessed—thanks in part to habitat and to prudent management by the tribal fisheries department—of legendary giant trout. The pothole lakes of the Blackfeet Reservation grow rainbows ten pounds and bigger. The reasons why are all history. Prior to the Ice Age, this part of North America was a vast, shallow sea. As is the case in all seas, living organisms, like plankton, that photosynthesize the sun's energy lived and died in unimaginable numbers. And when they died, their tiny corpses fell to the sea floor and accumulated over the millennia in rich layers of sediment. Under the pressure of geological time, these sediment layers were pressed into rock, rich in what was left of the tiny beings—nutrients like phosphates, magnesium, potassium, and calcium.

This is dry country. To the casually wandering eye, it appears sere. But the lack of heavy rainfall allows the earth to hold on to its precious nutrients. They didn't percolate away with eons of rain and floodwater. The vegetation that does grow, then, is hardy, laced with protein. The buffalo that once grazed here grew massive from the nourishment of high-energy prairie grasses. And where there is water, in the pothole lakes left behind by glaciation, you'll find a boondoggle for aquatic plant life, which in turn provides luxuriant habitat and food for aquatic insects. Scuds, for instance, grow thick and meaty, like little popcorn shrimp for trout. And the trout grow huge.

There may be small fish in these lakes, but you rarely see them. At Duck Lake one spring I watched an endless procession of black silhouettes sweeping the shallows along the shore, their shadow-shapes set off by the strange, almost glowing aqua of the water and the wet-white cobbled bottom of the lake as they were hidden by the wind stripping waves across the surface.

I fished scuds to the Duck Lake rainbows. It was too early in the year for the prolific damsel hatch, and I found the scuds much easier to throw than leeches and Woolly Buggers. The wind, the horizontal panes of air rushing at me, made much of my decision in favor of scuds as well. I chose pink over green or brown. I stood thigh-deep in the water, crouched to reduce my profile against the slanting early morning sun, and waited to spot the fish cruising in the strange, bright blue water. I found them working in broad hoops, or figure eights, floating by me at regular intervals. I timed my casts to allow the scud to sink before the fish reached it, then retrieved with two halting strips broken by a two-count pause, trying to place the action in the direct approach of fish. But on each circuit the trout, while predictable in their general routes, redefined their course with sudden,

twitchy attacks on something new they spotted in their underwater realm, or with wary wrigglings to shy from some
sensed danger. Witched by intuition or desire, a vast majority
of my casts were never seen.

When I had placed one well, I could see the lake. The big
trout moved in eerie jerks, one moment in one spot, the next
a foot or so forward, or so it seemed because of the wobbly
light projected into the water between waves. One moment I
would see the white slash of a large trout mouth opening,
then a wave, and before I saw the strike, my line pulled
taught, throbbing with the shooting disappearance of the
hooked shadow into the depths.

I did not catch a multitude of fish that morning—a half
dozen only—but sight fishing made the action feel constant,
or at least the potential for action inspired every cast. And
then, honestly taped, the smallest fish landed was nineteen
inches, the largest twenty-six.

Another spring day at Duck Lake I fished the southeastern
shoreline, where prevailing winds pushed the wave action
and kept the gravel clean for trout attempting to spawn. Far
across the lake I could see colored dots standing or floating
along the shoreline, fishermen on the bank and in float tubes
hugging the northwest shore in an effort to let the wind work
with their casts. But there was nobody on my side. The lake
looked desolate. Walking along my shore I felt alone and vulnerable.

It's a well-discussed proposition in Montana that an unhealthy number of Blackfeet harbor a strong dislike toward
whites. Sometimes that dislike boils over into outright
hostility. Knowing this, the flat, hopeless cast you see in the

eyes of people staring at the beer coolers in convenience stores, their edgy anticipation of rejection when they ask if you will buy them a six-pack, is enough to let anxiety fizz the hair on the back of your neck. I don't have any Blackfeet friends, a fault of my own making. I don't have any windows through which I can peer into the lives of the people who live on the Blackfeet Reservation. Traveling alone on the empty, wind-beaten plains, I feel out of place. I feel the measure of eyes upon me—the way, I imagine, Blackfeet folks might feel when they travel alone into Cutbank or Great Falls. I feel a little afraid. I'm not proud of it, but to deny it in deference to political correctness seems to be as wrong as running away from that fear and hiding in the vast, Indianless expanses of our white country.

I don't know any Blackfeet people, but I go back to the rez hoping I might meet some. In the absence of knowing the people, I've made myself familiar with their history, their mythology, some of their customs. It helps me to understand why they might feel less than enthusiastic about buddying up to people like me. Dead white people loom like specters on most reservations, and the Blackfeet rez is no different. In the 1890s, having already destroyed the Blackfeet way of life, the U.S. government wanted to mine their land. When the tribe—ravaged by starvation, alcoholism, and disease—refused, the government threatened to cut off their supplies until tribal leaders agreed to allow the mine.

As late as the 1920s, people on the Blackfeet reservation were allowed to starve to death by our federal government. The Blackfeet—at that point only a generation or two away from their days as rulers of the high plains—had not conquered the American system of food production. Many of them depended on government rationing to eat. During the '20s, corrupt Bureau of Indian Affairs officials, skimming profits by selling beef designated for tribal distribution to whites off the rez, simply stood by and allowed Indians to eat their leather belts, hatbands, and boots in efforts to survive the winter. Hundreds didn't.

Even today the Blackfeet feel the weight of injustice. They feel, probably rightly so, that much of what we know of as Glacier National Park was in fact originally described as part of their reservation. Even more disturbing is the decade-long, multibillion dollar lawsuit against the U.S. Department of the Interior (DOI), filed by Eloise Cobell, a Blackfeet tribal member. The suit alleges that poor to nonexistent bookkeeping by the DOI allowed mismanagement and outright pilfering of billions of dollars—$137 billion, Cobell claims—for lease land, held in trust for Indians under the Dawes Act. When the trusts were set up, Indians were assumed to be unable to manage their own accounts. Instead, the government managed it right through its fingers—there's little doubt that the DOI is at fault in this case; the arguing has been reduced to how much the feds will eventually have to pony up.

Today's Blackfeet perhaps find some solace in the fact that they still live in this place of their ancestors, that there exists for them a biological, geographic, and spiritual continuum extending thousands of years into the past. The spine of the world still stretches across their western horizon. When I looked out over Duck Lake that morning, I saw Blackfeet men in many of the float tubes bobbing on the water, fishing with fly rods or spinning gear. I felt, too, a little prickle of doubt about where I was on the lake, vis-à-vis where they all were. So many other people seemed to be on the other side of the

lake, and nobody fished my shore. I thought my map said that
I had reached an open access point—there were no signs—but
I wondered if perhaps I was in the wrong place, on private
property, or tribe-only territory. I felt spooked—until the black
shadows cruising the shallows let me forget about that.

A friend had given me an experimental blood-leech pattern with a peacock hurl head, and although my initial in-
clination had been to go with scuds, the leech looked too
delicious. I found a spot where a draw in the lake bottom
dug a steep drop from the shallows, waded waist-deep, and
cast along the crest of the drop, stripping slowly. As I
stripped I looked to my right, to the deeper water. My nerves
were admittedly already jangly, so when I spotted a huge
fish—possibly the biggest living trout I have ever seen—
swimming dead-on toward me, the fish spooked the hell out
of me. It was big enough that, at first glance, I was scared to
be in the water with it. I froze, breathing deeply, and the fish
veered. I tried a cast as it angled away, but the specter
vanished, unassailable.

A few minutes later, I spotted two trout working in the
deeper water and stripped the leech in front and to the left of
them. One of the fish whirled and attacked without hesitation
and the fight was on. The fish banked out of the depth, over the
crest of the cut and into the shallow water, its shoulder throwing a V wake behind it. Then it turned and sprinted back, dropping over the lip and into deeper water again. I backed toward
shore, losing some line, and fought the fish in ankle-deep
water. Eventually its runs described short, fast, half-moon arcs
through the water in front of me until I dragged it to my feet.
This was a healthy fish, nineteen, twenty inches, but nothing
like the monster that had startled me earlier.

After I released the fish, I noticed a battered brown pickup truck bouncing down the rutted dirt road to the shore, and I noticed again how keenly alone I was. Once more, I feared I might be trespassing. The truck slid to a stop, raising dust, and both doors swung open. Two Indian men wearing jeans and nylon jackets stepped from the cab and stood for a moment, watching me as I started to cast as nonchalantly as possible. Then the men began walking toward me.

"Do I know you?" one of the men asked. I couldn't think of a reason why anybody on the reservation would know me. I looked at him for a moment, trying to find recognition.

"I don't think we've met," I said.

"You're pretty ugly for a white guy," he said.

"Well, in any case, I don't think we've met," I said.

"I don't think I'd forget a face that ugly," the man said.

I laughed to see if he was joking, but he didn't laugh. "Your name isn't Kipp, is it?" I tried. A guy named Kipp was the only person I'd ever met from the reservation. He was a guide from Browning, and I had met him when I was working at the Grizzly Hackle in Missoula perhaps four years earlier. He had walked in the shop with a thick stack of pictures, each of bigger and bigger trout taken from Duck Lake. He was the reason I started fishing the rez.

The man standing on the shore said, "Yeah, Joe Kipp."

"Well damn," I said, "We have met." I told him where.

"I knew I couldn't forget a white man as ugly as you," he said. This time he laughed when I did. We chatted about fishing conditions and he told me he was taking his younger cousin out fly fishing for the first time. I wished them luck, and the two of them headed down the shore.

I fished the leech to another gliding silhouette and hooked up. But after a short fight, the fish split my tippet and took my one-of-a-kind fly. I tried mohair leeches after that, but could not turn a fish. My glances down the shoreline kept pointing out that Kipp's cousin was hooking up fish after fish, although he couldn't seem to get any of them in. I didn't want to bother them, but obviously Kipp knew something I didn't. I walked down to where they were. Kipp sat on the bank while his cousin fished in hip-deep water.

"How you been doin'?" he asked.

"I lost my magic fly," I said, "Haven't done much since."

"Still using leeches?"

"Yeah."

"Leeches don't work too well," Kipp said. His young cousin hooted as he hooked up another fish, then promptly lost it.

"You guys seem to be going to town," I said.

"You need some of these," Kipp said, digging into his vest to pull out a box. He spilled three or four very sparsely tied orange scuds.

"Yeah, you know," I said, "I had some scuds but I left them in goddamned Missoula."

"Take some of these," Kipp said.

"Oh, I can't just take them," I said.

"Trade me something," he said.

I lifted a fly box from my pocket and poked through it with my finger. "I have these nice articulated leeches," I said, showing him the jointed pattern. "Good action in the water."

Kipp snuffled, then said, "Sure I'll take that. Some client will think it's pretty. Now these scuds, you want to think of basketball when you fish them. Think of the fish's mouth as the hoop and just try to drop it right into them."

I did what Kipp said, thinking basketball, and when I dropped those scuds onto a trout's nose, the fish tilted up and ate. I caught eight more hefty trout before leaving the lake to start the five-hour drive back to Missoula.

The night before my most recent trip to the Blackfeet lakes, I lay on the bed in a motel room in East Glacier, intaking Henry Weinhard's and Isabel Allende for a while before sleep came. Eventually, though, I had to switch my TV on and turn it up loud to cover the strange sounds coming from the room beside me. There were two Indian couples in the adjoining room, making more noise than I thought possible—irregular eruptions of thumps and cluds and whomps, but not one single word or laugh or moan. Not one voice.

I knew they were Indian couples because I had seen them earlier that evening, hauling voluminous bags full of wine coolers and Miller beer into the room. The two couples were—and I'm surmising here—in town for the North American Indian Days being held in Browning. Earlier that evening, the Goat Lick Lodge lounge had been full of Indian couples two-stepping to country songs, friendly couples who all seemed to know each other and who appeared to take some pride in their dancing.

In my room I wondered what was happening next door. I did not know anything about those people in there, any more than I did the people I saw hunched up against cinder-block buildings in Browning, or the couples sliding their heels across the floor at the Goat Lick Lodge. But with the people in the motel room beside me, I wondered if something was going to happen that might make me find out more.

I turned the TV up to hear a *Saturday Night Live* "Deep Thoughts" segment that went something like: *for an Indian, shooting an arrow into the back of a pioneer woman and watching her fall to the earth must have been the greatest thing to do.* It was an amazing irony for me in my room in East Glacier, already nervous about something I didn't understand. Then, precisely at midnight, all of the disturbing noises from the room beside me fell away with the drifting, tailing regression of a spring rain blowing itself out.

In the morning I headed down the long road to Mitten Lake. As I drove, my eyes were drawn upward with the sweep of the forested mountain front to high, shining cirques and rock ridges curved like incisors. I would not have been the least surprised to hear that grizzly bears ambled from the wilderness on the shoulders of those ridges to the lake in the bowl below me, or to know that silver wolves slipped silently along its night shore, kneeling to lap the cold, moonlit water.

I rigged my rod and float tube and put in. I kicked against the wind, which was wild and searching enough to swirl down into even this protected bowl and cover the lake with riffled crowds of small waves. I positioned myself about twenty yards deeper than the obvious drop-off on the lake bottom and cast back toward shore. The first strike came when I was off guard, kicking to reposition my tube against the wind as I stripped. It had been weeks since I fished a streamer, and when it happened, the slight hitch at the end of my strip did not register. It wasn't until the long, jiggly tug that I knew I'd been struck. And then I held my fish too tightly.

The flight of the trout on an opposite vector from the recoil of my stiff 6-weight rod parted the leader at the fly knot.

I collected my line, snipped my tippet, and tied on a stronger section, knowing that hadn't been the problem. The problem was I hadn't quite trusted myself to let go soon enough. It wasn't a new thing; it was a very old one that I would have thought I'd be over by now.

There would be more trout, of course. I understood that. Still, I took a moment to wonder how big the fish I had lost was, what it looked like, where it went. But on this day, somehow, as I sat in my tube holding a broken piece of line, the rez and its trout seemed to be taking their measure of me, instead of the other way around. It's not a feeling I would want every day, but this afternoon it came to me honestly.

Brothers in Waiting

TEN-YEAR-OLD TALAN STANDS slightly spavined on spindly legs in the grass along the banks of the spring-fed pond. He squints in the bright Montana sunlight from beneath a baseball cap that looks three sizes too big. The squint pops his buck teeth. The cap protects his scalp from the sun. I met Talan half an hour ago. I don't know his disease—leukemia, neuroblastoma, Ewing's sarcoma, Hodgkin's—I don't know his prognosis, where he is on the curve. I don't ask; that's not why I'm here.

I know that in his ten years, Talan has found out more than most of us will ever know about how sickness feels, and that, on this clear afternoon, he wants to know how something else feels. He wants to know how it feels to wave a fly rod in the air and shoot a line straight over the water and, possibly, to hold the sudden, livid pulse of a fish stretching that line in his fingers. I want him to know these things. I wonder if he can understand that this is as important to me as it is fascinating to him.

With my arms wrapped around him from behind, my forearm pressed against his to keep his wrist straight, I listen to Talan telling me he thinks that fly fishing is the best because the flies look like real bugs. Talan has been talking nonstop about other kinds of fishing he has done. He wants me to know that he's done these things.

If I had the opportunity to trade never catching another fish for Talan hooking one on a fly today, I would. But we're not catching anything. "All those paddleboats scare the fish," Talan says. He points to the plastic boats churning merrily around the pond, carrying counselors from Camp Mak-A-Dream and other youngsters like himself, all sporting bright yellow life jackets. The way Talan talks about the paddleboats and the fish makes me again aware that he is wise beyond his years. "We're not going to catch any because all the fish are down in the deep water," he says.

During the summer before I entered the eighth grade, my mother and father and my eight-year-old brother, Chris, left me with a family friend for few summer days while they drove two hours east to Cleveland. These were days like any other in that summer before eighth grade, days of riding bikes, throwing footballs, bologna sandwich lunches, then maybe fishing for bullheads below the dam. Except one late morning I remember my father reappearing alone, waiting in his blue station wagon. Through the rolled-down window he said, "Come with me."

"But we're going to play putt-putt golf," I said.

"Come with me, you can play putt-putt later," he said. We drove only a block and he nosed the car into a gravel pull-out at the park across the street from our house. There, with the summer breeze soughing through the leaves of tall oak trees, my father told me that my brother was very sick.

"He's going to die," my father blurted. Even at the age of twelve, I could tell that he knew no other way to say it. The helplessness spilling through his voice as he spoke out the windshield at the sunny morning made me as scared as I was stunned by the thought of my little brother no longer living with us.

The doctors gave my brother five years. They had never known anyone with his disease, an extremely rare congenital disorder called Fanconi anemia, to live much longer. We waited. My brother was immediately introduced to a course of experimental drugs. These drugs did horrible things to him throughout his youth, in a time of his life when nobody should have to face horrible things.

The day I fish with Talan, my brother is twenty-nine years old, and although the edge has dulled, we are still waiting. We are thrilled that we can. None of us know how much is left, only that Chris is, right now, very much alive. And Chris does everything he can to remind himself of that. I never taught my younger brother to fish. Standing so close to Talan, I wonder if I have taught my brother anything. I learned so much about my life through him, but I wonder if there is anything of value he had taken from me.

Talan, like all of the kids at Camp Mak-A-Dream—kids suffering from cancer and various blood diseases—have brought nothing on themselves. They're just kids, and, on this afternoon in their lives, they want to be fishing. Talan wants to learn fly fishing.

"Hey you know what I wonder?" Talan asks when I'm try-ing to show him how to strip a Woolly Bugger. "I wonder if I could just reel the line in."

I try to tell him that reeling it in means he'll have to strip it all out again to cast. He reels anyway. Then I realize that the metaphor of that process, gaining all the line on the reel, stripping it off to cast, maybe that kind of procedure doesn't seem so tedious to him. He's got all afternoon this day. It's a different kind of patience, a graceful acceptance of time.

Later I switch Talan to a Turk's Tarantula. On his second cast with the dry, I see a fish cruising the banks turn and zero in on the fly.

"There's one," I say, "See it? Hold still."

Talan sees the fish and I can feel him stiffen, waiting to jerk the rod on the take. I crouch behind him, hoping to soften the impact somehow, feeling myself tense as well. I want the fish to take so badly. With each stroke of its tail carrying it closer to the fly, the shape of this fish comes clearer in the pond. "He's coming," Talan whispers.

The trout flicks away at the last second, but swirls be-neath the fly, still looking up, its flanks lucid flashes of light in the spring water. *Take it!* I hear in my head. *Take it, take it, take it!* My hands hover, poised and trembling, not touch-ing Talan now, not wanting to distract any of his senses from what is happening. He leans his bony body forward, soft eyes wide open, buck teeth popping from his gaping mouth. His fingers grip the rod. He leans. I lean. The fish tilts. I can feel Talan's breath catching with mine. We are perfectly balanced, me behind him, the fish under the fly, and our potential is un-limited. For this one flash of a moment, while we watch the trout, Talan and I become brothers in waiting.

Blue Moon, Blue Sharks

THE NOTION AT HAND was records, world records, in particular the fly-rod bluefin tuna on twenty-pound tippet record. I'd never thought much about records, not about holding one, anyway. In fact, I sort of loathed people who chased them. But then Dodd put a bug in my ear about how easy it would be to break the twenty-pound tippet record, which at the time was thirty-two pounds. "That's just a little football," Dodd had said over the phone. Over the phone, Dodd's generally a little more certain than he ought to be. But he's infectious. I scheduled the first seven days in September to break the mark. That this is a little like scheduling a year, say, 2008 to win the Pulitzer did not occur to me until later.

The hurricane was still a faraway thing, a tiny little storm buzzing westward off Bermuda, something named Emily. How much trouble could something named Emily cause? How many Emilys got called to the principal's office? How many got caught smoking pot?

This was how I tried to talk to myself, whereas underlying the boosterism, I was already beginning to understand the problem. During the phone call in which world records were discussed, Dodd had goaded me into some sort of offshore fishing orgy off the Rhode Island-Connecticut coastline. The tuna—yellowfin, bluefin, and albacore—had been milling south of Block Island for weeks Dodd said. It would be only a matter of days before they started slashing the surface. He said dolphin lurked under any floating object—lobster pots, jetsam, seaweed gobs—and were striking like airline mechanics during the holidays. White marlins tipped their bills at trolled teasers. Stripers and bluefish blasted the inshore reefs. The time to strike was now! The day to fish was today!

Which is what talking to Dodd is like. And then he would temper it with something like, "Hey, if we get nothing else we'll stay out on the water all night and fish for sharks."

When I arrived in Rhode Island the sky was clear, but swells from Emily, still cruising the North Carolina shoreline, tossed the ocean up the breakwaters, and a warm, wet wind coated the coast. For four days I sat at Dodd's house in Stonington, Connecticut, and watched the neighbors' flags leaping from their poles. I listened to cycle after cycle of the dull, crackly marine forecast, hoping for a break, but the offshore report remained remarkably consistent. On Thursday it was no different than it had been on Monday: winds twenty to thirty knots, waves five to ten feet. Thursday was definitely a wash. Likely Friday as well. My flight departed the following Monday. Which left nothing but cocktails and which explains why *Big Game II* was in the picture.

For the most part *Big Game II*, which belongs to Dodd's brother, Jon, is a fine boat. It's a twenty-three-foot SeaCraft— a 1979 hull, one of the best made—that sits up on its chines and carves the top off waves, In fact there was absolutely nothing wrong with the way *Big Game II* ran the seas as we cruised across tilting swells, leaving far behind the dusky line of shore, seeing nothing but sunset and the broad expanse of empty sea and, in the far distance, the Block Island light.

All traces of the storm were gone, replaced by a calm so flat that only the boat's forward motion created breeze. Dark began filling in from behind the sunset. We anticipated, in the weather's wake, heavy fish activity. Our plan was to chunk for tuna all night, listening to the radio and reports from the commercial boys. If by morning we hadn't set the record, we'd chase schools until we did, then maybe knock off the mahimahi mark, too. And, if nothing else, there would always be sharks.

The water temperature, sixty-eight degrees, was nearly ideal—sixty-five would have been perfect—but more important, this was early September. Blue sharks migrate in spring and fall. They arrive in New England in large groups in late May, when water temps hit the high fifties, then disperse over the summer. In September they begin to congregate again in preparation for traveling south. At this time of the year the sharks are aggressive, attempting to jack up fat reserves for their long swim.

We were heading for Coxes Ledge, a drop in the bottom contour from twenty to twenty-five fathoms. We were thinking tuna but not oblivious to the fact that, like so many of us, sharks seek structure. Currents rake ledges and ridges in the ocean floor. Schools of fish, traveling along the ridges for cover, pile up in heavy currents where the sharks hit them. We were not terrifically concerned with tides, although a full moon—a blue moon, in fact—would shine some night light for us. We cruised eastward, thirty-one miles from America, almost to the ledge. We were looking at high hopes. That's when something was wrong with *Big Game II*.

The engine locked up. We sat adrift as darkness rose like a mist from the sea. Jon pulled the engine cover from the mechanism, monkeyed with it for an hour or so before announcing a monosyllabic verdict we already knew.

"Dead."

With the Mariner 200 died my tuna record. I sat on the port rail and watched as darkness began leisurely completing itself, leaving only a swath of lighter gray on the western horizon and a dome of brightness to the southeast, where the moon was beginning to rise. In the total absence of wind I felt moisture begin to condense on my face, and I felt too disappointed to be worried about the fact that I was adrift at sea with the Dodd brothers.

Which was probably why I allowed myself to be talked into doing something most people would consider not a very good idea, given the circumstances: setting up a shark slick.

Dodd, Jon, and I sat on a small, disabled boat—a boat stocked full of chum—parked in the dark thirty-one miles from shore but smack in the middle of shipping lanes, and decided to attract large marine predators. We did have the wherewithal to radio the Coast Guard to let them know we were out there. This was my idea, which initially met with resistance from Dodd and Jon who worried the Coast Guard might send someone to rescue us forthwith and really get in the way of our fishing.

"So let me get this straight," the Coast Guard officer said, "You're disabled, but you're not asking for assistance?"

"That's correct," Dodd said.

"Can you stand by for a moment *Big Game*?"

After a long pause the radio crackled again and a different, fuzzy voice said, *"Big Game?"*

Dodd's eyebrows lifted. "We got the Big Cheese now."

"Here's the way we see this," the Coast Guard Big Cheese told us. His tone was dubious. "If you're not calling for assistance then all we can do is call anyone you'd like us to, or we can invite assistance for you."

"We don't want assistance," Dodd said. "We were going to drift and fish all night anyway, so we've decided to go ahead and do it."

"Is there anybody you'd like us to call?"

"Well, if you want to keep our wives up all night—"

"Would you or would you not like us to call someone?"

"No sir."

We agreed to radio every half hour and announce our continued survival. Then the commercial towing services from Point Judith, Block Island, and Mystic began ringing in and for a while we felt like the best-looking girl at the dance. We dickered before arranging a daybreak pickup with a tow service from Block Island—$800 it would cost us—then we clipped the radio and the spotlights off, to save our battery, and we sat back and waited.

Jon had already started a chum bucket and had rigged several deep-sea bait rods, dropping the baits back into the slick and slotting the rods in holders around the boat. The bright blue moon legged up over the ocean's horizon. Fog gathered inches from the water's surface. I tied a leader, rigging a few inches of twenty-pound wire tippet.

Back on shore during the windy week, while the hurricane had kept us dry-docked, Dodd kept dropping mention of possibly attracting sharks with our tuna chunking. As my frustration at not being able to get on the water mounted, he had encouraged me to peek at the International Game Fish Association book under the blue shark heading. Sitting in his house with big tumblers of Gosling's rum and ginger beer, Dodd was already trying to skim the bubbles off the slowly fizzling tuna trip. He started saying things like, "You never know with tuna. If we find them, you'll get your record. But you never know if you'll find them. Now sharks, I can guarantee you we'll get into some sharks in excess of one hundred fifty pounds . . ." Which, I had noticed in my peeking, was well above the twenty-pound tippet class record at the time, a mere eighty-nine pounds.

That number began to bleed over the tuna record in the forefront of my mind as I sat in the dark on the powerless boat with nothing to do. The wind was so dead that our slick built all around the boat, coating the hull in a foul film of decomposing marine flesh and fish oil. We waited for the tide to spread our chum. The building fog closed out the distance so that everything we saw was right in front of us. Dodd kept telling me that you never know what might follow the slick, that we weren't out of the tuna hunt yet, although to suggest that he'd already tested the limits on my suspension of disbelief would be the nicest thing you could say.

Yet the night held still as a spooked breath, and the cool white fog hovering around us seemed strange enough to let me wonder. While I waited in this small sphere scrubbed out of the fog, I realized I wouldn't know what was coming to us until it was right there. Suddenly the sound of slapping pebbled the water off our stern, as if somebody had cast a handful of rocks into the sea. Everybody leaped for a rod, Jon and Dodd going for midweight spinning rigs.

"Those are bonito!" Dodd said, gripping a spinning rod, poised to launch a popper into the night.

"Where are they?" Jon asked.

"I don't know. I can't see them."

"Where the hell are they?"

Dodd popped on a flashlight, sweeping the water with it, but the fog clogged the cone of light only a few yards out. Then the peppered splash sounded again, off the port beam as the bonito chased bait. Jon whipped a popper blindly into the fog and reeled, working the lure with quick jerks. I reached for the nearest streamer, a squid pattern, tied a quick, lousy knot, cast, and started stripping while the night returned to silence. Our buzzing reels, slushy strips of line, and game-time breathing were the only sounds the fog bounced back to us.

We sat back and waited again. A chilly film of moisture coated every surface of the boat. "The secret here," Dodd said, and I perked up, thinking I might at least learn some sea lore, "is not to let your underwear get wet. That can ruin your night."

At the stern Jon chopped a flat of mackerel into chunks and plunked them overboard. The moon climbed higher, peeking at us over the edge of the fog layer with a cool, chalky hue. Then quickly the moon stepped free of the wall of fog, showing us a clear slice of indigo and starlight overhead. As the night dragged on, we quieted, our bodies increasingly aware that it was now past one thirty in the morning.

Unwatched in the darkness, one of the bait reels clicked. Then click-clicked. Then six quick clicks. Then the reel let out a short scream. Dodd, who was wearing the fighting harness, ran to the rod, lifted it from its holder, fit the butt into the harness cup, and waited for the line to move again. When it did, he snapped the drag, hit the fish hard twice, and reeled.

"Bluefish," he said, clearly disappointed.

All around us reels started clicking and screaming. A school of bluefish were slamming our baits. I listened, trying to imagine the school in the dark water below the boat, mercury glints as the flanks of the blues whirled in attack. Dodd and Jon manned rods, reeling in a blue each.

"We'll bleed these," Dodd said. Back on the docks, Al Conti, who runs Snug Harbor Marine, suggested I soak flies in blood to attract predatory fish. Besides, I thought it might be fun to fight a big ocean blue on the fly rod, so I cast the streamer, watching my yellow line sink into the liquid darkness while I let the fly gain depth. In two strips I felt the line slapped from my left hand and heard the reel sing. I hit the fish, but couldn't get a grip on the spinning reel handle. I tightened the drag, managed to grasp the reel, and hauled back on my rod. The line flew from my spindle.

"That's a shark," Dodd said, tearing the fighting harness from his waist to wrap it around mine. Before he could, my rod sprang back, the weight released. I reeled in. The hook on my streamer had been straightened.

"That'll keep the blues away," Dodd said while he rebaited his rods. Jon slit open the bluefish he and Dodd had boated and bled them into a five-gallon bucket. I dipped a new, marabou flesh fly with a mackerel-striped tail in the bucket of blood soup, then tied it on my leader. Dodd popped on his high-beam flashlight and weaved its light through the dark water close to the boat. We could see the nearest bait, dead white against a background of flat, dark depth. Then a shark cruised by, eerily sailing along in no apparent hurry. Dodd hit it with the beam of light and the big shark's sides lit up a brilliant neon blue, bright as any tropical fish. Only huge.

"How big?" I asked.

"Six feet, more or less," Dodd said. "You want to try him?"

"Should I?" Neither of us had a clear understanding of the capacity of the fly rod I had brought, a loaner from Orvis, versus a shark.

"You've got the harness on," Dodd said.

I stripped line to the deck and shook some off the tip into the water so I could load up for the first cast. On my back cast, blood from the soaked fly splattered my cheek. Jon and Dodd, sprayed as well, ducked behind the center console. I spun about forty feet of line into the air and waved it up there, raining bluefish blood all over the boat, while I waited for the shark to reappear. When it did, Dodd trained the light on the neon blue of its long flanks. I dropped the fly far in front and beyond the shark, giving the streamer time to sink so I could strip it directly under its snout. The shark wound a slow circle around the beam of our spotlight, black eyes bulging, mouth partially agape. I started slow strips to position the streamer.

The shark whirled in the water, slid toward my fly. I made two more long, even strips. The shark bumped my fly with its nose. In one flick of its tail, it bumped the fly from a completely different direction. I made another cautious strip, drawing the fly perhaps a foot from the blue curve of the shark's nose, drawing my breath tighter.

The fish rolled, opened its mouth, and sucked the fly into its gearbox of white teeth. The shark acted like this was nothing, an afterthought. Its tail pushed it forward in a glide. I slammed back on the rod. *Wham!* once. *Wham!* twice. The shark paid no attention, continued swirling in our slick, moving now to the outside ring of the flashlight's brightness and losing its garish blue glow, becoming instead a dark, fluid eddy and flow. I hit it. *Wham! Wham! Wham!* Then, like a guy at a bar who has been sitting too long without service— slightly annoyed, but not losing his cool—the shark got up and left. I watched bright yellow line peel from the big reel.

I knew it would be important for me to turn the fish at some point, and decided to try before it got too deep. I braced my thighs against the gunnels and hauled back on the rod, with every foolish intention of holding it upright to fight the fish. My attempt to turn the shark not only failed, it provoked the fish into a heartfelt run that slammed the rod to the gunnel, nearly hauling me into the drink, where the home field advantage would have taken a dramatic turn.

Line zinged from the reel. All I could do was watch the orange streak of the backing zigzagging across the shrinking spool, and keep my fingers away from it. The shark's power coursed up the line to make my hands grip the rod like an electrical current. An added kick came from the knowledge that, unlike, say, a really big brown trout, should I slip here and wind up in the water . . . well, the fish on the other end could eat me in the most gruesome fashion: alive. I fit the rod butt into the gimbaled cup of the fighting harness and sat back in the chair, fiddled with the drag, waiting for some indication that the shark was slowing. My backing spool contracted like a snowball in a bucket of boiling water.

When it began to slow, I turned the drag even tighter and hauled back on the rod. I held. Twenty or thirty more yards of backing yawned from the reel, and then the line began to slice across the sea's obsidian surface, showering the dark water with green sparks of phosphorescence. I ripped back on the rod and reeled frantically as I dipped forward again. Ripping and dipping I regained line for fifteen minutes. The shark was trying to rest, but I understood the importance of not allowing this and I could feel myself plowing its weight backward through the depths with every heave on the rod. The shark ran again, digging into its dive, and I held on, dipping my hips with the rod butt in my groin to reach a deeper fulcrum. Then I went about the process of gaining line back.

By the third run the tendons on my forearms popped where they joined my wrist, but we'd been at it for a half hour and the shark was losing steam. When again it entered the beam of our flashlight, it half rolled with the fluttery-eyed look of a bad athlete after a long run.

The shark surged once more, blasting two powerful sweeps of its tail to turn from the boat and root its nose for the deep. But, exhausted, it slid to its side. Its efforts from that point were concentrated on keeping itself upright and pointing anywhere but directly toward the boat.

"Male," Dodd said, talking to Jon who was scribbling information onto a tag he'd received from a shark study group. So little is known about where sharks go, what they do, where they breed, or give birth. Tagging is one small way to start finding out. "About six feet long. Hundred and twenty pounds. There's your record."

It was the first time since I'd hooked the shark that I'd thought about records. The tuna record had seemed like such a clean thing. A tuna we would kill to eat—weighing it first for record consideration would be sort of a formality. But slaughtering this animal to get my name in a book seemed so insignificant compared to standing on the boat in the foggy night, with the blue moon burning cool overhead, attached by a length of line to the surge of electric blue fish.

"Tag him," I said.

Dodd laughed in a way that made him seem glad that he'd escaped an embarrassment. "That's good because we don't have any way to kill him," Dodd said. "We forgot the gun, and we can't drag him behind the boat because we don't have an engine. I suppose you could jump in there and try to choke him to death."

"Let's just get him off," I said, thinking that in a matter of moments, both the fish and I would be off the hook

Jon brought the tagging stick to the gunnel. With a heavily gloved hand, Dodd reached over the side and grabbed the leader, careful not to let it twist around his wrist. Jon lunged at the shark, poking the razor-sharp tag into the cartilage at the base of its dorsal fin. The shark whipped into a berserk spinning frenzy, wrapping the leader into its gills. The line sank like slices into the shark's soft flesh, a strange sight, and I noticed that I was having a strange thought: I was worried for the shark's safety. This, I knew, was not something most people think about on a disabled boat at sea at night.

Dodd worked the leader around the big fish, trying to unwrap it, but the shark kept pirouetting, its mouth peeled away from its jaws to show raw, fleshy gums and the bone-white maw rowed with teeth. When finally the shark stopped spinning, Dodd unwound the leader. Jon handed him clippers, and he leaned far over the edge of the boat and sheared the leader just above the wire section. The shark sank away, kicking a few lazy swipes of its tail while still in our view, then regained strength, and linked together a number of tail turns that carried it into the blackness beyond our lights. I couldn't see how reading my name in a book, that transient little monument, could bring back the trembling I felt in my hands. I doubted any record could be clearer than my memory of the blue, blue fish sinking from my vision in that deep, calm place, that beautifully eerie nighttime sea.

Sharks, like most ocean fish, are overfished and some populations are nearing collapse. Sharks' legendary, if unearned, reputation for savagery—"the perfect killing machine," someone once called them, although a tuna is pretty good at killing what it wants to eat, as is a trout for that matter; and we're leaving people out of the discussion—siphons sympathy from sharks and leaves them vulnerable to witch-hunt mentality. Meanwhile, scientists are just beginning to understand how vital sharks are to healthy oceans. A 2005 study, one of the most complex and thorough ever done on marine ecosystems, illustrates the cascade effect that shark exploitation has. Sharks act as a check on midsized predatory fish like groupers and jacks. These species prey on the grazing fish, like parrot fish, that keep coral reefs clean and healthy. The depletion of sharks, the study's authors—Jordi Bascompte and Carlos Melián of the Estación Biológica de Doñana, in Sevilla, Spain, and Enric Sala of the Scripps Insitution of

Oceanography—noted is partly responsible for the shift in Caribbean coral reefs from coral-dominated systems to places where the primary plant life is algae.

Still, sharks are caught in numbers we can only guess. In many cases, fishermen slice off sharks' fins and dump the animal back into the sea, alive and helpless, wounds gaping and open to the salt water. In the Pacific Ocean, Asian demand for shark-fin soup has sent all major shark stocks reeling. Atlantic populations are not much better off. What regulations exist for commercial shark fishing are rarely—if ever—enforced.

Shark populations are diminished enough that even the recreational trophy fishery, which focuses on catching and killing the biggest of the big, can be harmful. Dodd, Jon, and I fished for sharks all night, and the fish kept our action steady and serious. We never knew when a mako might cruise our slick, or a great white; we heard on the radio during one of our periodic check-ins that a bunch of great whites had been spotted feeding on a whale carcass about ten miles from our location, and that kept us on our toes. We tagged fifteen blue sharks and lost three or four others before the blue moon set and a dim light began to lift the hem of night fog in the east. We flicked the radio on again in time to hear the beckon of the towing service, already under way from Block Island.

We dumped what was left of our chum. The morning brightened, and the fog receded somewhat to open up a middle distance where the water rolled gently, like muscle working under a satiny gray-blue skin. Our flashlight no longer penetrated the ocean's surface, and we could only imagine what huge fish sliced silently through the cloud of chum and chunks we had dumped off our stern.

Slough Creek

FISHING WAS NEVER MEANT to be a contest, although what finer way to put your buddies in their place? That is to say: everybody's keeping count. When I headed into Slough Creek in September of 1993, I was going in to outfish—or at least not be outfished by—Phil Adams. Sure, there was an early-season backcountry elk hunt going on, which was why my father and his buddies were there. I'd tote a rifle, tromp the hillsides among the blackened pine skeletons, but my hunting would be impaired by little visions dancing through my head, images of tall, dorky, redheaded Adams slogging through the water, head a little hanging as he asked me, "So . . . whatcha catching 'em on?"

Adams is—I think this is right—nine feet five inches tall, with a face full of unbridled, rust-colored hair. He would look good sheepish, or cowed. At least I think he would, I've never

actually seen him either way. He's got a marriage of convenience with shame. I've seen Adams explain to the uninitiated
about the famous fly pattern he invented, describing it elo-
quently, in great detail, and without the slightest hint of guilt.

Establishing how I met Adams seems important; nevertheless, after all these years I can't recall. What I know must
be true is that Adams was taking classes at the University
of Montana where I was in graduate school. For a number of
years Adams came over from Columbus, Montana, in the
winter, when the backcountry was inaccessible. He took
classes like the rest of us watch cable TV: if he happened
upon it and found it vaguely interesting, Adams sat through
it. He took -ology classes for the most part—biology, geology,
hydrology—with no rhyme or reason, which explains why, at
age thirty-nine, Adams is still technically a freshman. But
he knows a lot of stuff.

Adams's real life happens in the Beartooth plateau and
the high hills and valleys that fold away from it. He grew up
there. In the spring he rides into the mountains with his dog,
Friday, and whatever one horse will carry. He sleeps on the
ground, eats what he can find or catch, and bathes sporadi-
cally in streams. He collects shed elk antlers to sell to the
Traditional Chinese Medicinal market, where they're ground
up as aphrodisiacs. He finds new raptor feathers to stick in
his beat-up felt hat. He lives decidedly on the lam, avoiding
nothing other than the rest of the world.

Montana, in general, is the land of the home growns. This
is a state where you see bumper stickers that say "Gut-Shoot
Them at the Border." Outsiders are not suffered gladly. I am
an outsider. Adams is as homegrown as it gets. That never got
forgotten when I first started hanging around with him, and

even while we were largely doing things we both appreciated—fishing, throwing retrieving dummies for our dogs, walking tiny spring creeks for a peek at some ruffed grouse or perhaps an ermine, singing "Will the Circle Be Unbroken" at 3 A.M. in his sister and brother in-law's driveway—Adams always assumed he knew a little more about what was going on than I did. It was not as if no learning happened. From Adams I learned to distinguish a hawk from a falcon on the wing. I learned how to start a campfire in the pouring rain. And I learned how not to run a wooden drift boat into a bridge abutment, although this was a lesson Adams apparently hadn't completely mastered before teaching it to me.

Slough Creek was exciting to me because of the stories Adams told. He talked about grizzlies snuffing around camp after dark, northern lights massaging the night sky, elk bugles flexing and floating from the dense forest, and fish—golden trout in the high mountain lakes, dumb little cutthroats in the creek above the falls. Farther down, just across the Yellowstone Park border, the fish supposedly grew bigger.

Part of the allure, I'm certain, was that this was Adams's home water. We fished the Bitterroot and Rock Creek when Adams was hanging out in Missoula, but those were streams I knew almost as well as he did. Slough Creek I'd never been to. Granted, we were not expecting to deal with fat and savvy spring creek trout, but we were going to be surprised about some of the challenges we found.

The ride in took most of one day. Myself, my father, and a few of his hunting buddies jiggled along on horseback for eight hours with Pete Clark, an outfitter from McLeod, who was going to show my father and his friends how to shoot elk.

We were going to meet Adams in the bush. Somewhere along the trail, the forest turned from the various dark greens of pine and fir to an endless burn, a spooky cathedral of thick stakes, charred and slanted, with the sun crashing through to create a contrast between yellow grass and blackened trees.

For a long time I simply could not look into the burn and see anything other than black and monochromatic yellow. In fact, as we rode, I spent a while looking directly at a particular arrangement of dead, burned downfall and stumps before I realized that what I was seeing was a cow moose standing a few yards off the trail.

We passed through miles of burn, the many small knolls of the valley visible where they would not have been before the trees were denuded. We crossed Slough Creek three or four times. Then the valley flattened into broad meadow and, in an island of live trees—this small grouping that somehow the fires skipped over—we spotted Clark's camp.

Camp bespoke the business of outfitting. Five or six canvas wall tents with pine log stanchions flanked a lodgepole corral. Between a pair of tents, a tree platform held boxes of food high above the ground to discourage bears. Littered around camp were woodpiles, shovels, axes and rakes, a bucksaw, lariats, cinch straps, breast collars, panniers, tarps, lanterns. Sawed-off logs circled the campfire, serving as stools.

And standing in the middle of it all, a giant geek wearing the same jeans and plaid shirt he'd had on for a month, a battered cowboy hat, a pair of black Chuck Tanner high tops—his "Tenny Llamas"—and spurs, smiling like he'd just built the whole camp himself, was Adams. We clapped backs and he spoke in his deep, booming voice and I, frankly, felt too

whipped from the ride, too creaky in the knees, to do anything other than stand around and watch while he and the
wrangler, Bill Dugan, put up horses. Dugan, a tall, burly
Irishman with a hint of strawberry in his blond and a touch
of boy in his face, walked around barefoot in the spongy,
green manure coating the floor of the corral, whispering
sweet nothings to all the horses. Adams and I chatted, caught
up a little bit while we readied for dinner. Adams, it turns
out, was having problems. He'd taken to limping almost as
soon as we arrived. Suspecting skullduggery and a possible
sandbagging, I opted not to mention it. But after watching
Adams limp around camp for a few hours, my father, who is
a doctor, said, "What are you limping for?"

"Aw, my foot's all stove up," Adams said.

"Let me look at it," my father said.

Adams peeled off his Chuck Tanners to let my father see
that he suffered from an ingrown toenail, which, left to fester
for a couple weeks, had built an infection that bloated most
of his foot.

"Jesus Christ, how do you cut your toenails?" my father
asked.

"I just cut them in the dark with a knife or my teeth or
whatever you do when they're putting a hole in your sock."

"Well we've got to do something about this or you're going
to lose your toe."

Adams didn't disagree.

Fortunately my father travels prepared for such emer-
gencies, and the following afternoon a little surgery was held.
Dugan, the wrangler, was drafted to hold Adams down. A bottle of whiskey served as anesthetic for both Adams and
Dugan. "Hey I can take a gallon of pus out of a horse's ass,"

Dugan said when he found out he'd have to preside over the operation, "but just show me one minute of that surgery stuff and I'm throwing up."

The whiskey bottle emptied, surgery proceeded apace. Dugan jammed a piece of wood in Adams's teeth and held his arms down. Margie Clark, Pete's wife, held Adams's leg, and my father sliced open the toe with a scalpel and dug the toenail out. It wasn't quite that simple. There was screaming and writhing, too, and several kinds of name-calling.

Later that evening, after wandering down to the creek to fish, my father and I went to the cook tent to visit Adams.

"How you feeling?" I asked.

"Oh fine," Adams said, woozy with booze.

"You have any throbbing?" my father asked.

"I'm a throb-free individual. How 'bout you? You throbbing anywhere?"

It was two days before Adams was able to ride again, and during that time I hiked rims and high mountain bowls surrounding camp, spotting mountain goats and bighorn sheep on the rocky peaks above me, never worrying about getting lost because I could always climb the highest ridges and see the mile or so of meadow below. When Adams was ready, he and I rode south through the meadow, through the woods to the stream, which gathered itself to make a deep cut into the hills, dropping off a series of rock ledges and a waterfall.

After that the trail opened onto the Silvertip Ranch, the only piece of private property within hundreds of square miles. The Silvertip sits just on the edge of Yellowstone Park, and we diverged from the main trail, circled around the ranch, and crossed over the border into the park by what Adams called the "Poacher's Trail." I didn't want to know how he had come to know the Poacher's Trail, although I would guess that he'd ridden it late at night as fast as he could before.

Just inside the park, Slough Creek is a meadow stream, snaking back and forth across a broad, flat valley that opens wide into golden hills with benches and aspen turning so brightly yellow that they seem to quiver. Above the aspens vaulted rimrocks. The September sun lay low against the ridges to the west, casting a glow on the grass of the valley. Grass shadow colored the trail a blue groove. The wind blew hard, tossing the tall stems, and then like magic, as soon as we slipped off our horses and started joining rods, the wind stopped.

I felt acutely aware of the openness here, given the woods I had been hiking and riding through all week. One of the elk hunters in our camp had, the morning before, walked up on a grizzly. I realized that if I saw a grizzly here on Slough Creek, I would see it coming from a long distance. Even so there would be no way I could make it to the distant trees, and so the bear would have a leisurely time of it, figuring out what to do with me.

The water of the creek was beautiful, flat and clear with a slight green cast to it. In the slow runs, long trout held against the undercut, outside turns, their forms greenish shadows in the water. And they were actively feeding. All around I heard the silence of the big open punctuated by *glip, glop, glip, glop, gloop*—trout sucking bugs off the surface.

Adams and I fished side by side for a while. I supplied him with a rod and his choice of flies. When I thought he made the wrong choice, I didn't let him know about it. Adams hadn't cast a fly rod all summer and at first he had a line-management problem: the excess line he stripped out to cast kept tangling on his spurs. But he actually hooked the first fish on a Stimulator. Before releasing it, he held it up momentarily for me to see—a big cutthroat, much bigger than what we had been taking in the upper stream.

Unburdened by knowledge, I remained convinced that Baetis Emergers were the way to go, and I fished them without dressing. I found the trout remarkably selective, blessed with a long look at my presentation in the flat, clear water. The water was so clear that, when my first strike came, I saw the trout tip up from the bottom, drift back, tilt its nose under my fly—and it was too much. I set the hook long before the fish got its mouth on it. I moved upstream and found a run of faster current where the river bent and poured over a shallow gravel bar. I could see fish on the gravel bar with their backs out of the water, piled on top of each other as if they were spawning. But they were feeding and here, where they had less time to look at my fly, I started catching fish on almost every cast.

These were all cutthroats, strong, sixteen-, seventeen-inch fish, thick through the shoulders. They were deep fighters, not flashy, but serious about it—I don't care what anybody says about lazy cutthroats, these trout did not want to be hooked—and when I lifted each fish to look at it, I could see its fat, golden belly. I raked cutts in, noting and gloating slightly that I was within clear sight of Adams, who caught nothing after his icebreaker. I eventually sauntered back and offered up some small Blue-Winged Olives—Adams wanted nothing to do with something so fancy as emergers—and I wandered downstream.

The wide open of the meadow, the vibrant yellow of the aspen, and the fat bellies of the cutthroats occupied me. The fun of watching a new stream unwind before me, each turn revealing a novel set of circumstances, absorbed my focus. In no time I lost track of Adams and completely forgot to make a contest out of the day. I fished hundreds of yards of stream, taking big fish all the way. It became as marvelous a day as I could remember walking around in. Then Adams caught up with me and told me we needed to think about heading the several miles back to camp. We'd have to ride part of the way in the dark as it was.

"Well?" he asked.

"Well what?" I asked, oblivious in the reflection of this wonderful meadow stream.

"How many?" Adams asked.

In a fishing contest, it's bad practice to let yourself get outcrafted like that. You never let the other guy ask "How many?" first, because then you're stuck with the number you proffer. Whereas he can just lie.

"Seventeen," I said.

"That's a pretty good day," Adams said.

"How'd you do?" We were both smiling now, and he had lifted his cowboy hat from his head to run a hand through his red mane.

"I had a pretty good day," Adams said and shook his head once. I grinned and nodded and that was all that anyone said about it.

We reached the canyon section of the creek just as darkness set in, and after that, as we rode I could see sparks fly in the night from the shoes of Adams's horse. The moon rose full and lit the rimrocks all along the valley, shining so brightly that it created moon shadows as deep as daylight shadows, and I could clearly distinguish the tight plaid pattern in Adams's shirt fifteen feet ahead of me.

Adams talked about other times he had been back in Slough Creek, other years. He told me about parties at the Silvertip that ended up skinny-dipping with the summer girls who worked there and smelled faintly of horses. He told me about seeing the northern lights dancing across the sky above the meadow. He said seeing that will make you believe again. When we rode into the lower end of the camp meadow, Adams said, "Coming into this meadow is just like coming home to me."

We had, I realized, long before entered a contest that neither one of us could lose, and when this round of it was finished, I was simply thankful he'd invited me home with him.

Bitterroot River

THIS WATER HOLDS THE redolence of leaky poker hands and those songs haunted by nostalgia—neither are really solid ideas, but under certain circumstances you're going to play them every time. On the Bitterroot, the circumstances are neither melancholy nor desperation, but a big, fat, juicy stonefly hatch. OK, maybe it's a touch of desperation, too.

I often hate the Bitterroot. Or, to be politically correct: I fear that which I am ignorant of, and I don't know poop from soup about the Bitterroot. I know people who sing this river's praises as if it ran with their heart's blood. I swear at it and call it dirty names.

But even I recognize the Bitterroot's potential. Plenty of twenty-plus-inch Bitterroot trout eat dry flies during a certain season, though that season may last only three or four good days. When you catch the hatch, it's . . . well, it is sort of spectacular.

Coming as it does at the end of winter, presenting the first floating hunks of protein to fish awakening from the numbed slumber of the cold-blooded, the Skwala hatch provokes trout into madcap acts of foolishness. For a few days, there is no finer fishery than the Bitterroot—low, clear water punctured by tipping heads, brawny fish sucking down bugs like Jersey cops at a spaghetti social. Good luck figuring out which days those are going to be.

Even if you live on the banks of the Bitterroot, the window of opportunity is small. It opens as winter dies, when the spring sun melts valley snow, but before the high-country runoff begins. Water temperature has to warm enough to inspire nymphs waiting to crawl onto the banks. Rain can ruin everything, wetting the wings of adult skwalas, or raising water levels, which, even when clarity remains good, tends to put Bitterroot fish off.

You'll need a couple consecutive nights where air temperatures remain above freezing. Other variables include water releases from Lake Como, a reservoir on the river's West Fork; rogue snow squalls; and the fact that the warm weather needed to activate bugs will also precipitate more runoff. It's an elegant algorithim and when it's over, it's over. Runoff rages and you're done until June.

Timing is a sticky wicket when you live right here, when you can watch the weather day by day and sip coffee in the fly shops and beer in the guide bars and act on twelve hours' notice. I can't imagine planning a trip to coincide with the skwala hatch. I guess people try.

If there was a phrenology of rivers, the Bitterroot's intellect would lie in long, deep pools, its instinct along the steeply cut and crumbling banks. The Bitterroot is an unstable river by its geological nature. With every runoff it chews its banks, dragging additional trees into its course, sweeping away congregations of others. It changes channels, hops beds with the hard-driven savoir faire of college sophomores.

Undercuts, root balls, and logjams along the banks provide trout with the overhead cover they instinctually seek. But these banks are skittish, flighty. You have to know which runs have been stable long enough for fish to set up in, and which are—no matter how sexy looking—just too new.

Holding water is a more profound indicator of fish. Trout seeking protection from dive-bombing ospreys and the lancets of herons gather in the scoop of deep pools. There, food flows by in steady streams. Too, pools tend to stay where they are.

Did I say that I hate the Bitterroot? I've heard the river called bewitched, but many have been the days I'd gleefully strike the second and third letters right out of that term. I long ago gave up fishing the Bitterroot except during those few magical days—whenever they occur—of pre-runoff.

This was not so much a matter of never catching fish. The frustration came, rather, in fishing a section of river that yielded a bounty of sixteen-and-up-inch fish, then the next time out, under identical conditions, yielded all the beer in the cooler and nothing more. No other river took so long to solve, and so I caved. Lately I have wanted to get back to this water, to understand why it is so different. This spring I cheated and fished with guides.

There exists along the Bitterroot River a unique sub-species of guide, the Bitterroot Guide, an insular group that fish primarily these waters, guides who gauge the nuances of the Bitterroot in ways the average person, the average guide even, never will. Bitterroot Guides are the solvers of enigma, the keepers of secrets. They are eminently talented, some-what godlike, and no doubt a pleasure to fish with, if you go for that sort of thing. My problem is I can't take them as se-riously as they, with their Sherlock Holmes pipes, silly Har-ris tweed hats, and generally foppish postures, seem to ask to be taken.

So, while eschewing pure intellect yet trying to operate within the phrenology of the Bitterroot, I chose guides of in-stinct. I floated the lower Bitterroot on a Tuesday in mid-April with Matt Potter. I met Matt a few years back, during my own brief guiding stint. He was the Grizzly Hackle's head guide then, although he's since opened his own shop, the Kingfisher, also in Missoula. Back when we first ran around together, Matt was sticking lime wedges in his ear while he pounded shots of tequila, then tossed the lime at the pretti-est girl in the bar. Matt is six feet six inches with the face of a ten-year-old spitting watermelon seeds. You might imagine the spectacle.

Those were the bad old days, and much, much, much has changed, and yet certain foibles, certain habit energies en-dure. For instance, although there exist dozens of perfectly adequate skwala patterns—flies tied using materials and col-ors that actually resemble skwalas—Matt insists that Bitter-root fish see far too many standard skwala patterns. He fishes the hatch only with No. 10 or No. 12 Goddard Caddis. It's harebrained, but it works.

The day before we hit the river had been, by all accounts, the beginning of the blitz, the prime skwala days. Matt and I wasted no time. We launched his pretty little Stu Williams skiff at the Bell Crossing bridge. Matt recognized unproductive water and blew through those stretches to set me up at the cutbanks where current slowed and strung out in seams curling around fallen trees or dipping into grassy pockets. Fish waited everywhere we looked for them, one fish after the next, mainly lanky rainbows, recent spawners hot to recover protein. Matt was calling takes, saying, "Your fly's going to be eaten right about now," so I would concentrate and coil. Then Matt would bellow, *"Hit it!"* startling the living hell out of me as I tried to react to a take.

I nevertheless managed to set up a lucky streak, zinging nearly every take, and then, naturally, blew the big one, the trip-fish. Matt and I both saw its boxy head break the water with the casual cruelty of a confirmed predator. Matt bellowed. I flinched. We both watched as I struck back and my leader filament went *ping!* I, for one, knew it was as big a river trout as I'm likely to see on the surface.

How much longer the Bitterroot can possibly hold out as a producer of prodigious trout is anybody's guess. During the 1990s, the last decade for which information is available, the population of Ravalli County, which pretty much contains the entire Bitterroot watershed, grew 44.2 percent, one of the fastest growth rates in America. Stack-a-shack housing developments stud the valley now, and bigger ones, including at least one six-hundred-fifty-unit cluster bomb, are skating through the approvals process. Ravalli County residents have always been quite proud of their cavalier disregard for regulations and restrictions. On the Bitterroot,

new trophy homes crowd right up against the banks, drip-
ping septic leach and lawn pesticides right into the gills of all
those pretty fish.

By Wednesday, the Bitterroot had fished furiously two days
in a row. I booked Pat Berry through the Grizzly Hackle. He'd
been the hot guide in town so far, bringing in a twenty-six-
and-one-half-inch fish, a twenty-four-, and a twenty-two-
incher even before the hatch hit full swing. He wanted to take
me to a section of upper river that was hard to guide because
of numerous portages, but would work for an ex-guide like
me, and an ex-guide friend like Eric Ruberg—guys, in other
words, with low expectations of guides.

I'm not as familiar with Pat as I am with Matt, but I do
know that, besides being as good a guide as anybody working
the area, Pat's a talented painter and musician, and sub-
stantially comical once you get to know him. Less than a half
hour into our float he took to calling me Willard and my fishing partner Marge Johnson—even though my fishing partner
was named Eric Ruberg.

But Pat worked us, too, constantly cajoling us to pitch our
"junk" closer to the banks. Fishing the skwala hatch, you
can't put your bug too close to shore. Pat thinks that, as the
obvious seams see heavy fishing pressure, trout slip closer to
the bank—away from drift boats—and work almost imper-
ceptible lanes only a few inches into the current. It did not escape my notice that both Pat and Matt alter their fishing
patterns in response to the heavy pressure people put on
these fish, and I felt a little depressed about it. It would be
nice if we could restrain ourselves a little, leave some rivers
alone a little bit more often.

That Pat called our flies "junk" didn't faze me, because he'd devised the things, and they looked like junk. Pat had been drinking too much beer and experimenting with foam when he came up with something he called the Wing Thing and something else he called the INF (for It'll Never Fish)—which was in spirit a Chernobyl ant modified for skwala season. The patterns resembled Power Rangers more than trout flies, but fish ate them with delightful indelicacy.

Eric (Marge Johnson) hates the Bitterroot as much as I do, although he'll fish it more often in any given year. Marge feels he needs to be humbled now and then. But Marge and I boated a slew of fish with Pat, doubling up with uncanny frequency, particularly along the lower ends of riprap and rock banks. Pat had us slinging our junk into subtle slots in the nearly motionless slack of deep pools, which consistently produced cutthroats. On my own devices, I would have fished more obvious water, caught nothing, swore, spit in the river, and rowed off. I landed a toothy, twenty-inch brown, and Marge and I brought in dozens of fat cutthroats in the fifteen- to seventeen-inch range.

At the end of the float, a rain began to fall. It grew heavier and continued for the next two days, blowing out all the rivers in the area. Nothing would be fishable again for months, until, perhaps, the salmonfly hatch in early June—even that was a crapshoot, prone to the vagaries of rain and runoff. The window had opened for a few days onto a wonderland of big-bug, dry-fly fishing, then it slammed shut again.

Before the rain, standing on the banks of the Bitterroot, tired from a great day on the water, Eric and I stood beside our rigs for a moment before driving home. Eric—he was back to being Eric again—said, "I feel like I actually accomplished something worthwhile, catching that many fish, you know, on the Bitterroot."

"You know what I feel like?" I said.

"What?"

"Now I don't have to go back to that damn river until next year," I said.

But the gusto was rubbed off of that, and I think we both looked at the water, about to swell with rain, recognizing that if we had another chance to float the Bitterroot, say, the very next day, either one of us might just leap at it.

Keepers

ON MARTHA'S VINEYARD ONE late-spring evening, I rode with my friend Steven Dodd and a group of fishermen in a van to the house of Buddy Van der Hoop, a sort of modern-day Queequeg. We had come to the Vineyard to fish Menemsha Pond and the herring creek Buddy managed for the Wampanoag tribe. Dodd's tales of fat striped bass lurking at the mouth of the creek waiting to slurp down outwashing herring fry built an excitement I could not contain.

Later in the evening, Buddy would unearth family heir-looms, fuzzy early-century photographs of Indian men perched on the prows of catboats, poised to spear marlin. He would recount tales of spearing seventy-five marlin on one trip. The photos were beautiful, edges fragile as dust, the shadowy faces spinning the sort of nostalgic mystery that sometimes makes us all wish we were born fifty years earlier, when things were simpler and the fish were bigger.

But what struck Dodd and me most about our visit to Buddy's house was something we found just as we arrived. The van turned into Buddy's long driveway and swung us dangerously close to a telephone pole. As we swept by, I saw the huge, weathered heads of stripers past nailed to the pole, mouths agape, the leathery texture of the sun-cured skin and yawning eye sockets lending a spooky sense of menace to the frozen gapes. The pole shot by quickly and, in our group, only Dodd and I saw the bass heads. Only he and I were left wondering about the stories behind them.

For years Dodd and I have chased stripers together, and we have compiled, as friends who fish together over time do, a stock of experiences that range from the ridiculous to the sublime. Our tales about these experiences, in turn, range from the ridiculous to the blatantly untrue. In the early days, Dodd's knowledge of the water, the range of his light tackle spinning gear, and his feel for the deck of a small dory in the rough-and-tumble current around the reefs of Watch Hill and Fishers Island Sound combined with my naïveté of the quarry and inexperience with fly casting from a pitching deck allowed him a level of success that simply embarrassed me.

And yet last spring, sitting in the lower reaches of the Pawcatuck River, I caught about twenty fish to his one. That the fish were mere slivers of striped bass, barely larger than the flies they took, I refuse to acknowledge as anything more than circumstance. We were both casting to the same things. Fishing is, of course, not a contest. But when one of us so outperforms the other, we can't help but let the other know how

we're doing, particularly since, for years, the drubbings fell
the other way.

And they still do, but I must say if Dodd is one thing
about his fishing it's magnanimous. Ever since we started
fishing together, Dodd was every bit as anxious to get me into
my first keeper bass on a fly rod as I was to tug it to the boat.
Years ago, he knew nothing about what flies I could try, what
actions I should work into my retrieves, or about the capacity
of my gear. Nor did I. When I first met Dodd my experience
as a fly fisherman was limited almost exclusively to the freshwater pursuit of trout.

But Dodd took the initiative to ask around. He made
some phone calls, put me in touch with some people who
knew some people. There were mistakes at first. Early on we
sought the help of a fly guide who owned a shop near the
Rhode Island-Connecticut border. He sold us a bag of wind.
We got even by making up a private sobriquet for him, Captain A. C., a relatively bad name invoking the physiognomy of
the buttocks. Later, while working a pocket of blues or
stripers feeding on the surface we watched, dismayed, as
Captain A. C. blasted his boat full bore into the center of blitz
after blitz before killing his engines, scattering even the food-
obsessed fish.

But Dodd eventually turned me on to the good folks at
Snug Harbor Marina and the Saltwater Edge, who proved in-
valuable in terms of knowledge and advice. Dodd arranged
Martha's Vineyard outings with Van der Hoop and other
longtime striper fly fishermen. We found what we needed in
terms of info, and Dodd and I doggedly chased fish, rising at
3:30 or 4:00 in the morning to catch turning tides and ideal
breezes. When I left the East and moved to Montana, Dodd

scheduled precious weeks off work to fit my return visits and we would buzz around the reefs and the rocks, he with his light tackle spinning gear, me armed with fly rods, until we found results. But, in the beginning, neither of us would guess how long it would take in terms of time elapsed before I met a keeper with a fly.

I met Dodd when I was twenty-five and living, coincidentally, at 25 Young Street in Newport, Rhode Island. Dodd was twenty-eight and living next door to me. When I lived at 25 Young, I was trying to reduce my life to a focus on detail. I was trying to freeze moments and examine them minutely, because before that I seemed unable to avoid the terribly careless rambling of sequence and consequence. I seemed unable to race around the room of my life in time to catch each accoutrement before it fell and shattered. I came to 25 Young after living on the beach in Hilton Head Island, South Carolina, and I came seeking still life. I tried hard to make it that, tried a narrowing of scope to this one street I could clearly define. I wanted to make this one place known and, therefore, real.

Young Street was a narrow lane running between Spring and Thames, one block only. My house stood in the middle of the block, a thin, green Colonial with a curve of Victorianism in the fragment of shake shingle roofing over the entrance. Dodd's house, much wider than mine, was painted orange. Beyond the Thames end of Young Street stood the wood buildings of the wharves, and then Narragansett Bay. The area around Young Street was known as the Captain's Village because when the port had been more active ship captains made their homes here. They had sailed the world and brought back trees from distant ports and planted these exotic trees around the neighborhood. All kinds: chinaberries and chinquapins; bantlings, balsams, and birches; sandalwoods and sandaracs; as if these plants would keep pieces of the faraway world in their lives.

However we first came to speak to each other, my friendship with Dodd grew through our mutual admiration of a certain young woman who lived on the corner of our street, a tall, blonde woman with trade wind blue eyes and a Cape Cod chin. My fascination, in fact, had roots deep in terror, though I didn't know it yet. Dodd and I would find ways to be sitting on our respective front porches at about the same time she walked to work—hostessing at a local tavern—in breezy summer skirts. She moved so effortlessly, and that kind of movement, I must have felt somewhere in my lizard brain, could blow up my still life.

In retrospect, I am surprised that Dodd found this time at all. His work efforts were then and are still both manic and epic. As often as not he slept on the floor of his office. He was starting a company then, he and his brother, Jon, and Dodd's eyes burned with a vision of the big picture, the great swirls and eddies of cash flowing through the system. I was merely trying to write. When we both watched that girl walking down the street, it was because I was gearing up to think hard about life again, and he had run home for a bite to eat, having not a lot of spare change for dining out.

We would sit and chitchat and when she appeared at the top of the street we would watch her long legs striding smoothly, her long hair flowing behind with the offshore breeze. Shortly thereafter Dodd would be gone, back to an all-night work session, and I would flip on the liquid green cursor of my computer. Had I paid attention to the hope in my heart, however shabby, I could have known something about the way I was doing things. But it would take a lot longer.

My first fishing experience with Dodd came at night, along the rock jetty of Point Judith, and the fly rod stayed home. We climbed down the dark, slick slabs of boulders jumbling the jetty, our feet disappearing in sharp-edged black crevasses between water-slicked rocks. When we found footholds near the water's edge, we hooked wriggling sand eels to our lines and plunked them into the outgoing tide. We let the eels find bottom and left our bails open.

When you feel the strike come, I was told, let the bass run with it for a few seconds, then flip the bail and strike back. My one and only bump resulted in a hookup and I followed the pulsing line over the rocks, clambering down the jetty toward its blunt tip, falling through cracks and slipping on the slimy darkness. Before reaching the end of the jetty I landed a long eel of some sort that we never did identify, a twisting, knotted mess trying to turn itself inside out in an effort to disgorge the hook. I let the eel go. Dodd's brother, Jon, hooked a thirty-six-inch striper. He killed it.

Later Dodd and I would go winter flounder fishing in a spot so secret even the flounder didn't know about it. Fishing with Dodd, my fly rods would land spider crabs and blue sharks before my first keeper striper. I would experience the rush and mayhem of a bluefish blitz and parallel experiences with schoolie stripers before my first shot at a cow bass. Dodd and I were fortunate enough to be in the right place at the right time for one of the fabled May worm hatches on the Great Salt Pond. We fished frantically as all around us the swirls of midsized stripers bloomed amid acres of three-inch clam worms scribbled across the pond's surface. Each shallow pocket stuck to its own timing, and we reached four separate bays just as they erupted with bass. The fish we landed were all twenty-two to twenty-eight inches long, not keepers, but a boatload of fun amid the madness of their feeding.

By then the business Dodd had spent so many hours trying to get off the ground had taken off into a multimillion dollar concern. He had bought a house by the sea, married, and his wife had given birth to their first baby, a boy. His office hours remained manic and he faced the never-ending efforts of improving a house and raising a family. I had moved from Young Street to the Clark Fork River in Montana, fished nearly every day, eked out a minor living as a writer, drank too much with the careless fishing guides, and watched romantic relationships dissolve and fade to black in orderly succession.

Before all that, though, I spent my time at 25 Young trying to break things down to their simplest notions, trying in an aloof and analytical manner to live a life of carefully examined snapshots. I tried to see each scene and discern everything I could about what held it together, believing that if I could focus sharply enough on something, it could be made so clear that it would obfuscate the periphery. I needed to believe that if I could see everything as singular and alone, I could build my own unique relationships between each frame and myself.

But the world would not hold still. For summer evenings on end, I would walk to the wharves at the end of my street and sit out on the docks, trying to write the perfect description of sunset on the bay. Green-headed drake mallards and their orange-beaked hens glided atop a tide that waltzed through wooden pier pilings. On any calm August early evening in my lifetime the ocean slipping along the rock edges and pier pilings simmered. Then a breeze would chap the surface, breaking the reflection, racing in parabolic blue pockets across the harbor. The pockets spread and scattered, losing form.

But the real story went on below. If I was lucky it might swing by. If I was lucky, bluefish cruised into the harbor chasing bait. They would swim right in among the boats and erupt into a frothing feeding strike. First came whirled clouds of white birds, common and roseate terns, wings rowing in tight arcs. They dropped like wet snow, splashing to the sea where the schools of baitfish moiled the surface. The bait rushed from the depths to avoid the blues slashing at their bellies.

Bluefish blasted through the bait schools, shiny blue-black fish so focused on the upward pursuit of their prey that they flew out into the air at crazy angles, flipping over, splashing down headfirst, tailfirst, on their sides, or upside down. It looked as if somebody stood just below the surface and hurled blues out into the air. Then the feeding slick fell suddenly still, the harbor water dropping back to slack, the bird cloud dissipating. Only to explode a hundred yards away as the blues caught up with fleeing bait and the birds dropped in from the top.

Before long anglers arrived, a small fleet of boats drifting through the feeding slick, then hauling across the water after the next eruption. For as long as the blues stayed in the waters off the island their lives would follow these cycles, these blinding drives to feed that seemed triggered just before or just after slack tide as the sea began its next pull or push. But there was no predicting which tide, or where.

An algae bloom might concentrate baitfish and they would draw the bigger predators. Farther offshore, tuna hit the blues the same way. The feeding left no opportunity, no time, for details. Instead it burst forth vicious and willy-nilly, scattering across the rich blue of the evening bay. And I found myself watching the water, trying after each sudden stoppage to guess the next place where the big shining fish would shatter the surface and vault through the sky. This movement, I began to understand, must be part of my pictures.

I have a photo of my first keeper striper, a photo that Dodd took. Behind me the sky remains dark, only a shade lighter than the water. I am standing just inside the prow of Dodd's dory, cradling the bass under the jaw, my other fist wrapped around its tail. The striper's spiny dorsal stands erect, the webbing membrane between spines blue in the early morning light. My glasses reflect the camera flash, and my upper lip curls open with the effort of lifting the bass. The fish, too, holds its mouth agape.

It is a big fish, longer than the thirty-six-inch limit on the books that year, and well fed. My first keeper, and I would catch another one fifteen minutes after I slid this fish back into the dark sea. I caught these bass because Dodd took me to a pocket in the Watch Hill reef, a boil of current that looked no different from any other in the pull of tide over the ridge. But Dodd found his way in the dark to this exact boil, one rock among thousands unseen below us. He pulled a keeper off the first drift with his spinning gear. Then I drifted over with a fly.

The bass took and quickly stripped me deep into my backing. It ran first against the current that pulled our boat away from the reef, then turned and headed at right angles along the reef ridge. Any number of times I felt a steady surge of line and felt sure that the fish had wrapped me around a rock, that the line feeding out was caused only by the drift of the boat. But then the bass would abandon one safe spot and tear off for another.

The fish fought until finally it held still, and in the dying tide, I reeled us back up over its lair. And there we stayed for a matter of long minutes. Dodd was interested in how my Winston 8-weight would hold up, and in how big the fish might be. His spinning gear never noodled in the extreme horseshoe that he saw my rod describe, so he was overestimating the striper's size. I knew if I ever wanted to see this bass, I would have to trust the rod and lift. The water below me was cold and clear, and any number of times I raised the striper to a point where, in better light, I could have seen it flashing below us, could have gauged its size and known how excited I should be. Each time I raised it, the fish peeled enough line to dig in again on the bottom and we would each rest, ever so briefly, before beginning the process again.

These rests, although they could not have spanned more than ten or fifteen seconds each, were the moments that seemed to define the struggle. The fish and I held each other in one spot as the tide grew weaker and a grainy hint of light filtered into the eastern horizon. I imagined the bass down there, its fins working rhythmically to hold its place. The bass, too, must have felt the current slowing, but for brief moments that seemed to last for hours, neither of us moved. We concentrated on each other, holding each other still.

Until I remembered what to do and began to reel again, eventually bringing the bass through the cold, dark water and to the surface. Until I held it in my hands in the dark morning air and Dodd's camera flashed. Until I slipped the fish back into the sea, knowing I would never forget it and never see it again.

There is a picture of me with my second keeper, caught a few minutes later on that same morning, but it's missing the glow of a first fish. The second bass was smaller than the first, and I now had a better understanding of what my rod and tippet would put up with, so this one came much more easily and quickly to the boat. My face, in the second picture, is missing the intensity and the irony implicit in the first. The strained smile of that first photo spoke as much about the giddy joy of catching my first striper as it did the giddy joy of my whole life at that point. It's a reflection of the smile on Dodd's face, too.

One night while I still lived in Newport, during that summer when I thought all of life could be broken into still-life vignettes, I sat in the tavern where the blonde girl on the corner of my street worked. Dodd was not with me. He was working, moving his mind through the night. The girl was not working at the tavern this night, and I was sitting, as I so often did, with a group of sailor boys and sailor girls and we were talking about hands. In fact, I was proposing that wouldn't it be nice if you could tell everything you need to know about a person from his or her hands. I was examining the hands of a boatie girl at the bar when in walked the young woman from Young Street, my tall, breezy girl with her sun-strung hair, and she happened to know somebody right in the middle of my discussion.

It was hard to smile without wondering how I was smiling. She looked at me then as if she had known me all her life or had never seen me before, and she held her hand up to me and said, "Do mine."

My gaze focused on her hand and I saw quite clearly her tan fingers, slender, tapered, at least an octave long. I placed my hand against hers. I felt her warm everywhere against my skin, but I felt her most in the place where we did not touch, in the hearts of our palms. I understood that I would never know this girl, that she would breeze through my life the way she walked down my street, that this was as close as we would ever come, me pressing my palm against hers. I wanted to hold it there as long as I could.

The next day I walked to the cliffs on the eastern edge of the island and found a cutaway in the sheer rock walls, a slope of jumbled rock, and I scrambled down to the water. From their base, the cliffs looked nothing like they had from atop. From the base they were sheer, solid walls shooting so high they tilted over me.

And the rocks I had seen, what had from above looked like a solid point of round slabs piled outward into the sea, were actually made up of many boulders. Although they appeared stacked atop one another to rise from the waves sluicing by, I knew in fact these rocks were coming down, crumbling pieces of a parent grid falling in huge porous chips to the ocean. Colonies of barnacles encrusted the black rock promontory, arrayed with the efficiency of a grater. Overgrown manes of slick seaweed suffused tidal pool between rock formations. The pool water felt sticky on my calves, as if in washing away it left on my skin a film itching with microscopic life: phytoplankton, zooplankton, algae, krill, protozoa.

The tide rolled in, huge waves booming against the rock-head, shattering, showering high into the air, and misting against the bright sunlight in a tinkling, chromatic fizz. Meanwhile water streamed away across the rock lattice like liquid crystal. Wonderful sounds rode each impact, the profound *ka-choong* of the wave bursting against rock, then the tingling, effervescent fizz. I climbed out to the very point, where a piece of rock larger than all the others knobbed the promontory and there I sat in the late afternoon sun while iced cobalt waves boomed around me, sometimes showering me, washing me in that film of microorganisms, sometimes splashing in my mouth so that I could taste the salt sea, the same taste as blood and rust.

I thought about the empty heat in the heart of my palm when I had pressed my hand against the woman's. I tried to remember the moment, frozen in time, but I missed it already and I thought, you can freeze all of life you want, but could that account for blitzing bluefish?

Waves endlessly furrowed toward me, slithering under the glint of sun in the distance, and the horizon line wobbled. As the tide advanced, the rock ridge sank deeper in the sea. Most of it sank from sight, leaving only the knob upon which I perched, but by then I knew I could stay as long as I wanted, could leave any time. I knew when I did go I could walk back safely, that, unseen, the rock lay only knee-deep below the swirling salt water, the cold cobalt whirling coolly around the posts of my shins, itchy with invisible life.

Rorschach Bluegill

Few of us shoot ourselves during the evening hatch.

—Jim Harrison

IT WAS THE CONSTRUCT, I think, that took me back to that place I was so tired of visiting. The pond lay surgically still, drawn to a fragile tension so tight that one fly cast upon it might shatter the entire surface. Walnut trees, their trunks shaved clear of lower branches, teetered like frozen grasps over the water. Banks of clipped green grass couched the pond. Everything about the place spoke of grooming and pruning. Not a detail appeared unprescribed, except for a pocket of weeds floating in the hint of backwater where, from the north, inch-deep current trickled down a narrow concrete sluiceway to feed the pond. I almost expected an attendant in a white coat to appear, skimming the weeds off before night-fall, or plucking rotted, inky walnut pods from the lawn.

I had learned to fly fish at a place in Ohio that looked something like this pond, a private club where a rerouted spring creek had been bent and twisted just so through handsome lawns, and then through a designated Beginner's Pond, before exiting the grounds. I was ten or eleven, and my father joined the club so that we might learn to fly fish. I'm not unhappy that I learned in such a place, even if the entire enterprise was artifice. I didn't mind because I had no choices. It was what I was offered.

Twenty some odd years later things had come round to this: at the end of an October afternoon I stood not on the banks of what has become my home water, the Clark Fork River in western Montana, but instead on the shore of a sculpted pond in a Kansas lawn, and I was tired of the humiliating madness that necessitated this flopping around in my past.

As if scheduled, the sunlight reddened and slid with hypnotic gravity behind the cover of shade trees, and fish began sucking from the pond's surface clever, concentric circles that looked for all the world like ellipses into the future. Fishing this pond was not my idea. My new roommate, Walker, wanted me to. He wanted to see if I could catch on a fly some of the maybe-mythical two- or three-pound bass he swore he took on spinning tackle the last time he fished here. I had quit caring about fishing weeks before, even before leaving Montana. To my friends and me, this sounded a signal depth of the trouble I had found myself in, a flashing siren about what was to come.

I didn't know how much stock to put in my new roommate, Walker, or his bass tales. Walker was half cowboy, half optometrist, and all hilljack, based out of Fort Smith,

Arkansas. He lazed on his side in the grass on the bank, propped by an elbow, closely monitoring what I would do next. As soon as Walker had heard I lived in Montana and did a little guiding and writing about fly fishing, he had telephoned Arkansas and hazed his wife into shipping the fly rod he was just learning to use.

I stared at the pond surface, unable to detect any hints of structure beneath. "Three- to five-pound smallmouths," Walker had said, "I caught about ten of 'em." He said "about tin of 'em." That Walker had fished here before was of dubious commendation. The reason Walker and I were roommates at all was because we were both in-patients on a psychiatric unit at the Menninger Clinic, just up the hill from the pond. Both of us had seen some part of our world come so completely unraveled that, as a response, we wanted very seriously to kill ourselves.

Oh, what do you say about deciding to kill yourself that can possibly make any sense? I'm not talking about a funky blue Sunday, or a frustrating week, those fleeting Well, there's always suicide flits of wist. I'm talking about a long-considered and ponderous decision to choose to no longer exist, to no longer move forward in time, to suspend the future. I'd thought it through nearly every day for four months. Mine was never a case of finding nothing worth living for; rather I feared that I did not and would never possess, intrinsically, what it would take to complete a viable life. I had written the sad, sorry farewell notes and schemed carefully so that nobody who knew me would find my body.

A week before coming to Kansas, while grouse hunting near the Missouri River just north of Three Forks, Montana,

I had pressed the butt of my loaded shotgun into the soft dirt of a cutover wheat field, leaned my forehead down to meet the cold, round kiss of the barrel, and reached to touch the trigger, to make sure I could pull it off. When I realized that I didn't mind the way the barrel rim bit into the flesh of my brow, I became fully aware that a part of me was fully capable of killing the rest of me.

Depression on this level is a paucity of imagination in the face of an imaginary deadline. I mean, there's a teeth-clenching, burning-urgent sense that things have got to get better, soon . . . but they don't. In June I had given myself to the end of September. As the summer slumped toward fall, it became impossible for me to dream up reasons why this living struggle should go on, why I shouldn't lie down and rest, because I was tired. Everything had become either/or and I was so goddamned tired.

Every other summer, I travel to Rhode Island to fish with my friend Dodd. Sometimes we go offshore, overnight, hook mostly blue sharks, bring them to the rail, tag the fish, and snip the wire tippets. This past summer the Dodd squad hooked a big mako, a nine-footer, over four hundred twenty pounds. They took turns fighting it for three hours, the shark slashing and surging, before they finally brought the fish, ex-hausted, to the boat. They decided to keep this shark, to make mako steaks, and to kill it they decided to drag the fish backward until it drowned. They lashed a line around the mako's tail and throttled up.

I was not aboard for this trip, but I think about that mako, exhausted, played out, the beautiful swimmer drag-ging backward through the blue ocean, choking in the medium of its vitality, smothering in the realm of its former life . . . I think a major depression must feel just like that drowning shark.

In my case the ante upped with panic attacks. It's seductive to try another hooked-fish metaphor to illustrate panic attacks, but my past comes complete with a more apt comparison. When I was growing up, my younger brother had a yellow cat. At about the same time I was learning to fly fish, my brother's cat developed epilepsy. The cat could always sense his seizures coming, and he would tear around the house, madly dashing in the hopes of trying to outstrip something rooted deeply inside him. And always the seizure would spring, the cat would quiver, twist, and spasm on the floor, spraying himself with urine until, mercifully, he lost consciousness. Those moments before the seizures now burn in my memory, flashbacks of watching the slim cat streaking through the house in absolute terror of what only he could feel coming.

Some people simply can't imagine a major depressive episode as anything more profound than a few down days, can't imagine how a thing like that could turn crippling. In tentative voices filled with all the care in the world, my friends and family told me sad platitudes. "Things will get better," they said, "just give it a little time." And I wanted to scream, *Don't talk time to me, I'm bleeding fucking minutes here.* Because, I can tell you, there is with depression a high-pitched pain like nothing I'd ever stood before.

At a place like Menninger's, everybody else on the ward already knows what it feels like, and that's comforting. They all know that hope has been reduced to the tilt of your head beneath the white paper cup filled with pills of all colors that you stand in line at a window to wait for. Yet even still, even at the hospital, occasion is provided for humiliation and misery. My first day in Kansas I was slammed by a panic attack while filling out admission forms. I wound up curled in a feeble heap, bawling and gasping on the floor of the admissions office. I writhed at ankle level to a woman who sat and calmly buzzed for assistance as she finished typing up the forms, as if simpering, quivering lumps of flesh clotted her office floor every day of the year. It's just impossible to feel real nifty about yourself after something like that.

C. S. Lewis wrote, "If you take nature as a teacher, she will teach you exactly the lesson you have already decided to learn." I wonder what crazy old Charlie Darwin would have made of that? One of my Menninger doctors told me that, by needing to see things a certain way to survive, we deny other things. As early as the first evening I fished the Menninger ponds, I could look at the water—even this pond born of backhoe—and watch fish rise and see that Lewis, pious fellow that he was, maybe denied something about nature-as-teacher in order to believe what he needed to about his God.

The first time Walker and I walked down to the ponds, I was fairly stunned that the staff let us traipse off toward nature unescorted. They allowed us to carry flies, which have hooks, which are sharp, whereas when I arrived at the ward, a large, muscular man had watched me unpack my belongings and took from me all remotely sharp objects, anything I might conceivably employ to perpetrate a suicide. He took my shaving razor, naturally, and my pocket knife, but also my nail clippers, even my tweezers—as if anybody has the heart to tweeze himself to death.

Walker's wife had sent him a fly box with three flies. One fly looked like a mosquito wearing a mink stole, and one was clearly meant to be a Hare's Ear. The third fly looked mostly like a cigarette butt. It wouldn't matter. These were bluegills dappling the surface of the pond, they'd eat anything they could suck through their lips. Walker's line had no leader, so I attached five or six feet of 4X tippet, which made for some ugly casting, but . . . bluegills.

Before casting, I glanced back up at Walker, lying on his side, propped up on an elbow as the grass grew greener and the sun sank red in the Kansas sky. A dissonant smile hung from his lips.

"Here's one," I said. "When do you suppose the things you can't go back to stop, and the things you do forever begin?" We were in a mental ward; we were allowed to talk this nutty shit.

"Never, probably," Walker said.

"See, because I seem to be living for this past? But it's a past I don't even believe in."

"Just cast, Montana."

"You're the one who wanted lessons," I said, "You come cast."

"Naw, hell I want to watch somebody who knows what they're doing," Walker said.

I thought that was an incredible thing to say to me at that point in my life, but I said, "All right. So then where would somebody who knows what they're doing cast first?"

"There's a mess of 'em coming up right out there in the middle," Walker said, going deep with his hokey-pokey Arkansas accent. But I pointed my chin to where the concrete spillway trickled current into the pond. Then I spun line overhead, fumbling with the unfamiliar flex of the rod, the clumsy turn in the lack of leader. Finding a rhythm over this darkening pond felt faintly familiar and yet airy and light, like a memory of something I hadn't done yet.

I let line slide through my fingers, growing more comfortable with each back cast until the fly began to sing smoothly through the evening. For longer than usual I stood and simply cast, listening to the line shooting through guides, watching my loop speed through that line as it reached over a glassy surface, wine-stained with sunset. I dropped the mosquito fly into the spillway. As soon as it slid onto the pond, a fish dashed up and *glipped* away with it. Accustomed to trout, I struck too hard and taught a bluegill to fly.

Walker hooted from the bank. I brought the fish in swiftly and knelt to cradle it in my palm at the pond's edge. It had been since I was a small child that I'd caught a bluegill, that I'd even seen one. I had long forgotten how beautiful the vivid swirls of green and verdant yellows bloom from the belly onto the flanks. The blue spot on the hard gill plate was so rich it shimmered like a dollop. I shifted the fish in my hand so that the light caught it from different angles, and I watched the swirling gill plates flow. I probably would have stared at the fish until I killed it had not Walker called out, "It ain't an ink blot, for Christ's sake. Throw it back."

I did not want to release the fish for exactly this reason: I had made no connection between the bluegill and an ink blot. I saw it as a fish with beautiful markings that I remembered from long ago, from my childhood, and I felt certain that those colors had not inhabited me back then.

I ended up at the Menninger Clinic because . . . well, does it matter exactly why? I could say I was there because feeling the barrel of a loaded twelve gauge on my forehead did not scare me. Or I could say I went to Kansas because, in a moment of clarity, from some sweet, sane corner of my mind I heard a frail voice crying, Um, wait just a second.

I can say with certainty that the precipitating event, the trigger to my panic attacks and the enormous suck of depression, was the abrupt loss of a relationship. I fell into a relationship with a young woman that felt as unexpected as it did beautiful, like someone lighting a candle close to my heart. She was from my hometown, my past. Passing time revealed substantial differences between my perceptions and reality, yet still I made the only mistake you can make with someone like her—I took her seriously. She returned the favor while it was convenient, then grew blithely distracted, and as I became more of an inconvenience, she hedged betrayals with deceptions until there was nothing left but some final humiliation, which she chiseled home with a cold clang that collapsed from beneath me the latticework of my admittedly already shaky belief system.

It shouldn't have, true enough: but everything changed.

At the end of my first week in the hospital, well before I was allowed to leave the ward to go fish the ponds, I sat in a second-floor office and gazed over the green lawns of the Menninger grounds and, beyond that, at Kansas itself. Through the window I imagined the sound of the wind washing through the treetops. I already knew the ponds were out there, somewhere on this groomed, fourteen-acre hilltop. I already knew that Walker's fly rod was en route from Arkansas. But I couldn't make myself care if I fished those ponds or even found them. I couldn't make myself care about anything. Instead I sat and listened to a psychiatrist who had spent four days running me through a battery of tests—

Minnesota Multiphasic Personality Inventory, Rorschach, various IQ and a few homegrown specimens. This doctor sat back in his chair and, with the prehistoric calculation of a crocodile, told me that clearly my recent emotional disruption had overwhelmed me with such feelings of abandonment and betrayal that it had started to interrupt my thinking. My thoughts, the doctor said, had grown peculiar, illogical, and idiosyncratic.

I wanted to tell him: No shit?

But one of the ways we set people up to fail us is to assume they know how to help, and anyway by then I had started to think about my every thought, to analyze all my responses, to self-edit ceaselessly. I was already disturbed, for instance, because Walker, who during med school had completed a psych rotation, told me all about how to take the Rorschach. "Just look at the ink blot and whatever the first thing that comes to your mind is, say it," Walker had said. "It's a butterfly! It's a typewriter! You know . . . whatever. But don't start looking real deep and finding a bunch of little shit. That's where you get in trouble." Of course he told me this after I'd already finished my Rorschach, after I'd been so proud of myself for spotting remarkably miniscule images huddling deep within the shadows of the ink blots.

Walker seemed to like it when I caught fish fast. For long stretches each evening I'd find a fish every cast. Eventually I'd started backhanding into tricky spots beneath overhanging limbs, or roll-casting into exact patches of open water amid the floating weeds, or I threw all the way across the pond to a specific riser on the opposite bank. I didn't think of it as showing off because Walker got such a genuine kick out of what was happening. He whooped with every hookup and laughed as I skidded the fish in. I was happy to entertain him for a while, happy to give him something to laugh about.

For a week we came to the pond every night, Walker and me, and we began to draw followers. A few of the people who were allowed off the ward wandered down to watch, everybody seated on the lawn, furiously smoking cigarettes. For me there was no resisting the comparison to the scene from the film *One Flew Over the Cuckoo's Nest* where Jack Nicholson as Randall McMurphy hijacks a bus and then a fishing boat, introducing his fellow "feebs" to the dockmaster as doctors from the state mental institution, "Dr. Cheswick . . . Dr. Taber . . . Dr. Scanlon, the famous Dr. Scanlon . . ."

The differences I found stark, to be sure, but quaintly ironic. Many of my fellow patients, a seemingly disproportionate number, actually were doctors. Others were architects and computer programmers and professors and entrepreneurs, all previously highly functional people, unlike McMurphy's cryptically wacky flock. But we were, too, all in our unique proximity to this pond because we had stepped perilously close to killing ourselves. That's a strange bond.

These were peaceful pieces of evenings, respites, mostly because a group of very sick, very tired people shared them. I shared with anybody who wanted the secrets of fly casting, and I shared in their shouted laughter when even neophyte attempts produced strikes. Secretly I think we might have shared, too, a jealousy of the hooked bluegills as we watched their futile but nonetheless fervid wriggling—jealously because, though they were thoroughly overmatched, the fish on my line at least had something real to fight, a tangible vector to resist. And we all knew each fish would be set free when it was over, something none of us felt confident saying about ourselves.

I spent five weeks at Menninger. In my time there I saw two wrist slittings on the ward and heard of countless other suicides and attempts. I listened to people, beautiful people, describe their condition in dirges, listened to them coolly discuss which were the best pills for an OD, what entry angle cleanly severed an ulnar artery. At one point a man placed in my palms the knife he had weeks before used to carve his wrists. It was, truly, madness. But, even though the white walls of the ward stood just beyond the green crest of the hill, nobody killed themselves or even talked about it down where the bluegills lived.

Long after I had given up hoping for one of Walker's bass, I returned to the pond to cast for bluegills. I watched their tail-dancing etch the perimeters of a rod's flex, the little fish outmatched but unsurrounded and lying back for none of it. With every livid tug on my line I could hear Nicholson as McMurphy cackling, talking to me, crying, "You're not a looney now, you're a *fisherman*!" Every time I paused to examine the swirling gill plate, the deep blue dollop of a fish about to slip its shoulders back into the pond, I could believe that. I could believe that no matter what else had changed, I was, still, a fisherman. It was the first thing, I realized, that survived.

The Grand Slam

I'VE BECOME OBSESSED WITH permit, and I think you should, too. Permit zip in from nowhere, ratchet your pulse up to throat-thumping levels, then ignore you like cats. Just as quickly they're gone. Permit can transform a sojourn to a sun-splashed country like Belize into a peak experience in a lifetime of well-planned endeavors. They just usually choose not to.

It's OK if you don't exactly know what I'm talking about when I talk about these permit. If you're like most Americans you're probably not real sanguine about Belize, either. You may think, "Hmmm, yes, Belize . . . sun-soaked tropical coast; palm trees arcing up from sugar sand beaches; One Barrel Rum tasting as sweet and smooth as vanilla cream soda without the fizz; a steamy, jungle-cloaked Caribbean-Latino banana republic somewhere, well . . . below Mexico." You got it.

I went to Belize to catch a permit, a bonefish, and a tarpon in one day to complete saltwater fly-fishing's grand slam. There are ten or a dozen places in the world where the possibility of a grand slam exists, and only three where that possibility is accompanied by any sense of likelihood: the Florida Keys, a stretch of Mexican Caribbean, and Belize. Nevertheless, traveling to Belize with the stated intent of landing a grand slam is about as dumb as going to one of these fantasy baseball camps and announcing your intention of hitting for the cycle against, say, Nolan Ryan. In other words, it could happen, but, honestly, don't be silly. Frontiers International, probably the foremost bookers of fishing adventures worldwide (and the company that graciously arranged for my trip to be comped so I could write about it for a magazine) estimates that less than 2 percent of the fishermen it sends to Belize manage to catch a tarpon, permit, and bonefish in one day. The company hastens to add, however, that over 80 percent of Frontiers clients traveling to the western Caribbean encounter "realistic opportunities" to catch all three in a week.

Fortunately, Belize is such a magical place that spending a week attempting and falling short of a grand slam could describe seven of the best days of your life. There's the fishing, of course, which is world class. The coast of Belize is offset by the second largest barrier reef in the world, 175 miles of coral formations and shallow-water snorkeling that dazzles the mind with its display of marine biodiversity. Then there's what's above the water. Inland jungles teem with ocelots, jaguars, tapirs, howler monkeys, coatimundi, iguanas, and macaws. From the ragged drapings of rain forest flora rise some of the most hallowed remnants of the ancient Mayan empire. Because all of these attractions exist within a few hours of each other, if you didn't become obsessed with permit, you could easily enjoy all of them in a week's time.

Bonefish

Quick history: prior to the 1960s almost all high profile saltwater sportfishing occurred in deep water, behind motorboats that trolled lures the size of small dogs. Your target fish then were primarily migrating giants with pointy noses, like marlins, swordfish, and sailfish. Next a few fly fishermen took gear designed for flinging to fish tufts of feathers no heavier than the average boot, beefed it up, and started plunking about in the knee-deep saltwater flats ringing the Florida Keys. They quickly identified a new trinity of revered species: bonefish, tarpon, permit. Some market-minded individual pondered the concept, and catching a bonefish, a tarpon, and a permit on the same day became known as the grand slam. Everybody wanted one.

When you're in Belize and fishing with a guide like Gilberto Accosta, all you need is a falling tide and you'll get your shot at the bonefish. "Shots" are a notion unique to saltwater fishing. Freshwater fishermen don't think about shots because they're taking them constantly, casting repeatedly to likely habitat. But the tropical ocean is a vast, energy-sapping place and blind casting is a waste of enthusiasm. On the flats, you only take shots at fish you see. Herein, also, lies the difference between sportfishing and sport hunting. When you make a good shot with a gun, the animal has no choice: it absorbs the shot. With a fly rod, you can make ten or a dozen of the best shots of you're life, only to be blithely ignored. In flats fishing, your best shot is only the beginning.

You take your shots at bonefish in the most shallow water imaginable. Lithe and bullet shaped, bones's shiny scales reflect all light, in effect leaving them the color of everything—or nothing. Even though the water is crystal clear, you see bones only as fish-shaped impressions of the myriad photovoltaic wavelets that crisscross the Caribbean shallows. Or you see their thin tails waving above the surface as they tilt their noses into the turtle grass bottom to root out shrimps or small crabs.

When things were slow on the water, Gilberto would announce, "OK, we go catch bonefish now." And we would. Gilberto's face features mixed Spanish and Maya blood. He bears a fair resemblance to the Apache leader Geronimo, which quells a lot of the enthusiasm for disagreement. At one point Gilberto had poled us along a shallow ridge that rose from nowhere, at the end of which some lobstermen had built a ramshackle house on stilts in the middle of the sea. We had seen bonefish spraying water as they chased bait into the shallows. The wind was howling, making casting a difficulty and poling no fun at all. Gilberto told me to wade across, fish the seaward side while he held the boat. I waded barefoot into thigh-deep water until I spotted a big fin cutting the chapped surface. I cast to this fish and stripped my line in, stripped and stripped, and the fish followed and followed until the fly was almost back to the rod and I thought there was no way . . . the fish took.

Bonefish accelerate like artillery, and this one rocketed over the flat and in a long arc back to the deeper blue water. I watched the line on my reel dissolve. The reel zinged, and a glistening spray shot from the line as it sliced behind the fish. As soon as I retrieved my line, we did it all over again. When I finally brought the bone to my hand, it proved fat and healthy, a seven- or eight-pounder with platinum flanks. After I released the fish, I waded back over the shallow flat and my feet left chalky swirls to mark my trek. A few hundred yards away this impossible lobstermen's house stood on pilings in the middle of the sea. It was a beautiful place to catch a fish.

Gilberto almost guided me to my first permit. One cloudy day off Ambergris Caye, he stared over a sea surface that had taken the luster of molten silver. "Permit," Gilberto said. "They are coming."

"Where?" I asked.

"Nervous water. Ten o'clock, eighty feet out."

Seeing fish is all part of the package. On the flats, wind and tide action push water around in a crazy colliding pattern of short wavelets, hundreds of thousands of triangular shapes bouncing off and moving through each other. When fish move onto the flats, water bulges in their wake, disrupting that fractal pattern—nervous water. It makes nervous anglers. A school of eight permit swam toward us, evinced by a faint moil on the surface. As they drew closer their shapes—long and lithe as seen from above—came clear, and I took my shot. A quicksilver flash lit the water as a permit twisted to pick up the fly. Being a lifelong trout fisherman, I lifted my rod tip high in a strike. The line swung back to me smoothly. The fish disappeared with dismaying speed.

"No, no, no!" Gilberto said. "You must strip slowly. You must feel the fish . . . my friend." He added the last in a softening tone, but I think he may have been disgusted.

Tarpon

Tarpon are enormously gorgeous, bucket-mouthed fish larger than the average adolescent. Look at the name: *Megalops atlanticus.* "Be brave, lads! It's the *Megalops*!" Tarpon do not attack people, but they are deep through the shoulders and chest, long bodied, and they could suck your whole head into their cheeks. Their flanks are clad in scales the size and color of compact discs.

During my stay I spoke to a man who had spent three hours fighting a hundred-plus-pound tarpon. *Three hours.* "I think both of us never wanted to see each other again," the guy said about the moment he brought the fish to the boat. These sorts of statements flummoxed Tim Cooper, a cheerful heretic who could give a flying fig about tarpon or permit, but who was being paid by a magazine to take pictures of the fish, the same magazine that was paying me to try to catch them. Fishing, Tim felt, was fine, but not very photographically interesting, particularly when, after our early luck with bonefish, I took to leaving all the permit in the sea, where it was logistically difficult to photograph them. Tim and I hoped we would find better luck with tarpon, which at least jump, when we left Ambergris and headed to the Belize River Lodge just outside of Belize City on the mainland. But first, lodge owner Mike Huestner immediately hired a driver to spin us down the Western Highway to see some Mayan ruins, which Tim was much more enthusiastic about.

Mike and his wife, Marguerite, are warm and gracious hosts, and Mike tells the sorts of endless fish stories that fishermen love to listen to. Mike told me that sometimes there are two-hundred-pound tarpon in the river just beyond the lodge's lawn. The lodge is lovely—the mahogany and ironwood in the dining room polished to a deep red glow—and the meals here so famously sumptuous that Mike and Marguerite are loathe to dine out. Geckos hang on the porch

screens, iguanas drape lazily over nearby tree limbs, mana-
tees sometimes grace the river's banks, and parakeets
screech in the canopy. What would be wrong, I thought, with
lounging here for a while?

The structures of Xunantunich, once a regional capitol for
thousands of Maya families, jut from the jungle with dizzying
power. The earliest construction here dates from 400 BC, although Xunantunich flourished around AD 600. Two hundred years later the Mayan empire was gone. We strolled
across grass fields, under which once lay the paved courts
where a savage ball game played out—a two-on-two match
wherein players used their heads, hips, shoulders, knees, and
elbows to deflect a ten-inch ball through a ring. The games
lasted days, sometimes weeks, and, in a practice only NFL
coaches in the salary-cap era could appreciate, the winners
were sacrificed, often having their hearts torn beating from
their chests.

I climbed *El Castillo*, the archetypical Mayan stepped
pyramid that housed the all-powerful priests. Herein once
dwelled men whose sole responsibility was the procurement
of knowledge—geography, astronomy, theology—a fascinating concept not duplicated even in our much ballyhooed Information Age. On its walls remain carved friezes, a lexicon
of symbols describing matters of profound import to tens of
thousands of people.

I gazed over the main plaza and imagined how it must
have once bustled with peasants hustling corn, beans, chocolate, livestock, musical instruments, bees for honey. Imagin-
ing another world supported by the stones beneath your feet
is a stunning revelation about the frailty of time, and a shock
to any belief you may hold of a copacetic present.

Permit

Take a round sterling silver dessert tray. Stick a black fork of tail on one side, and on the opposite side, the face of a small child, or of Dick Cheney. There's your permit. Hardly an imposing figure, I know, but they're deep keeled and fast twitch and, for some reason, a lot smarter than other fish.

I may as well address the fact that the magazine article produced from this trip was never accompanied by a photograph of a permit. I would like to blame the omission on winsome Tim, the young lad who was meant to immortalize my first permit in rich tones on film for casual viewing pleasure—with perhaps a background of cumulonimbus clouds towering above the pastiche of sea, building into the impossibly immense purples and blues of the Caribbean sky. My own face would be grinning like a mad despot as I gripped the cymbal-sized fish by its sharp, skinny black tail.

But I can't blame Tim. Permit are hellcats. During my stay in Belize, a very accomplished, if somewhat priority-challenged man from Idaho paid somewhere around $15,000 to rent from the Belize River Lodge a mother ship, in which he journeyed about the more remote cayes and flats off the Belize coast with the express purpose of catching ten permit in ten days. I've caught ten fish in an hour in Idaho. The very accomplished fisherman caught all of one permit during his lovely cruise. That I relate this aside at all is only by way of saying that these fish instigate madness.

Our Belize River Lodge guide was a pale-skinned man named Leroy, another shallow-water genius. The first thing Leroy did was seat us in his flats boat and motor out to a flat he'd rather I not name. "Lots of permit here," Leroy said. Within two hours we saw perhaps one hundred fifty permit, a huge school that approached in patrols of ten or a dozen, charged off, regrouped, and finally streamed past us in a roughly single-file line that took five minutes to sweep by. They all managed to leave without cracking the masks of indifference that permeated their attitudes about the crab patterns I chucked repeatedly at their faces.

In three days Leroy showed us so many permit. There was the platoon of permit suspended over a white sand spot. As my cast to them launched—but before it hit the water—the fish spotted me and split like a cartoon army. There was a squad of ten fish cruising along about forty feet beside us. To them I cast and cast and cast. They ignored me with the redneck insouciance of turkey vultures. There was the group of permit I saw running behind us and tried to whip a back cast at, only to have the wind-addled fly thwap into Leroy's chest. There were three permit just inside the reef that I flailed at, feeling the wind smack my hook into my own spleen—not once but twice. Wincing but still determined, I placed a perfect cast three feet in front of the lead fish, which it promptly disdained.

There was a group of half a dozen permit that Tim spotted, their saber black tails waving out of the water—fish that were actively feeding, not just cruising nervously about, just exactly the circumstances you pray for—except of course I was changing flies and not at all prepared before the nearness of the boat and the general mayhem with shouts of "They are there! Right there! *Right there!*" which spooked the school badly enough that the water leaped with their escape. I turned another fish, a nice, blunt-headed specimen, enticed it to leave its friends and chase my shrimp imitation for about fifteen feet before it remembered it was a permit and therefore superior to me.

Look, it's hard. When you fish rivers, the water is moving, but the fish are mainly holding still. On the sea, the water is moving; the fish are moving, twitching in random vectors; the boat is moving with the wind and tide; your cast is moving, pushed by breeze; and you're moving, bobbing, and twirling with the waves. Everything's moving and everything happens fast. With these permit each shot just grew more nerve jangling than the one before, until finally we gave up and went tarpon fishing. That, if you know anything about saltwater fly fishing, is a ridiculous statement. *We finally gave up and went tarpon fishing.*

Leroy took us to a scythe of clear sand lying submerged in about four feet of water, completely bare of the turtle grass and other submarine vegetation that covered the flats for miles around us. The bare swath, which he called Miami Beach, ran almost half a mile long and maybe a hundred yards across and seemed lit from below, a pale saffron glow beneath a moving skim of lavender waves. Leroy set up the little flats boat at one end of the sandy scythe and poled us along until a huge, dark shape sliced parenthetically from the turtle grass fifty yards away and began a meander over the bottom. As I watched this animal approach—a seventy- or eighty-pound predator casually interested in sucking whole fish into its mouth—I wondered if I really wanted it on the other end of my line. My fly hit the water, I made one strip and watched the five-foot-long monster snap open its downturned jaw and suck the hook into its mouth.

A tarpon's mouth is hard cartilage. You have to yank your fly line in your free hand like you're starting a lawn mower to set the hook. I gave the fish three good rips. In response, the water parted and the tarpon blasted into the air, a silver fountain of scales and splash. Because of the miracle of buoyancy, an eighty-pound tarpon exerts considerably less torque while underwater than it does in midair. The strategy, when a tarpon goes airborne and exponentially increases the stress on your line, is to lower your rod, to bow to the tarpon, create slack instantly. The fish launched itself clear of the water four times, each a new shower of silver against the aquamarine sea. I fought him for fifteen, maybe twenty, minutes, and then he was gone. A roll in the right direction and my leader parted.

After so much futility, it had felt good. Blood pumped through my arms. I had been *attached* to a big and wild beast, *Megalops*, connected by a stretch of thin line—until something as intangible as my lack of skills parted our ways. A less genteel person might describe my grin as shit-eating. During the fight, the tarpon had dragged our boat some distance from our starting point, so Leroy poled to Miami Beach, picked another giant shadow cruising the saffron strand, and I cast. Stripped. A flick of its tail jerked the fish forward. Stripped again. Another charge that slowed just short. I stripped until my fly was only ten feet from the boat and watched as the tarpon extended its mouth and inhaled the fly. I'm not sure which of us, me or the fish, was more google-eyed. Into the air launched eighty pounds of rattling gill plates and shining disc scales. After a few more leaps, the fish settled down and began towing us around the cayes, a very slow rendition of the Nantucket sleigh ride. Ten minutes stretched into fifteen and then twenty and we remained locked in our postures. The tarpon pulled away, occasionally changing directions, dragging us along. I held the rod and lifted and reeled when I felt any slowdown. Then something occurred, something mysterious and forever unknown that had, I feel, little to do with my skill levels, and I found myself once again separated from a large fish. I reeled in to find the leader intact, fly still attached—but about a quarter inch of the hook point had been folded completely over and flattened against itself.

I hooked four tarpon over sixty pounds on Miami Beach. That night, after a dinner of shrimp au gratin at the Belize River Lodge, I lay in bed, the overhead fan redistributing the cool air sifting from the humming air conditioner. Two or three glasses of sweet One Barrel rum warmed my belly. Geckos on the screen made a *chk, chk, chk* sound, while farther in the darkness woodpeckers hummed a hollow-throated warble. There was a whole jungle out there, crawling with black panthers and fer-de-lance snakes. Just across the lawn, a dark river poured out into a crystal clear bay that was pocked with mangrove cayes. In the dark, fleets of bonefish scoured the flats and silver tarpon hunted among the mangrove roots. My shoulders felt stiff. A blister had broken open on one hand and stung. For a little while I thought, *to hell with permit*. Until I realized they were out there, too, charging around like cavalry, and I knew just then that I'll be going back until I catch one.

Third Spaces

WHEN I FIRST WENT to the Tuamotus, a smattering of islands strewn in a broad arc several hundred miles northeast of Tahiti, I was stricken by the seeming insignificance of the land. Formed when volcanic islands sank into the sea, these islands are merely rinds of dry ground rising atop a ring of coral reef, surrounding vast, round lagoons. On the outside, the land is fronted by the reef's edge, then three-hundred-sixty-degree horizons of muscular, leathery blue sea. At their best, the islands may vault to eight feet above sea level. At their widest, the land is no more than half a mile across. Even the coconut palms and pandanus trees seem low, every-thing just holding on, ducking its head. When global warm-ing gets its way, the Tuamotus will be among the first islands reclaimed by the sea, and all the cinderblock and tin-roof shacks that islanders live in, even the fancy resort hotel on

Rangiroa, will become just more complex structures for coral to build reefs with. Lionfish, ornate as Queen Victoria with all her ruffles and lace, can hide out under cupboards, and octopuses will skulk in the toilet drains.

This was the fall of 1996. I was just a year out of the Menninger hospital and looking at the world with what seemed like brand new eyes. I felt like that break from normality taught me that there was no reason why, at any point in time, a fellow couldn't decide to see things differently. Everything looked up for grabs, and I could start from any point and build whole new ideas and then live in them. The Tuamotus seemed like an excellent place to try.

Inside the lagoon of Rangiroa—at forty-eight miles long by fifteen miles wide, the world's second largest lagoon—the water is calm, revealing shaggy coral formations and depth gradations like a prism bending only the greens and blues. It's deep enough here, over one hundred feet, for whales to use as a calving ground, and tiger and lemon sharks find plenty of space to satisfy their carnivorous wanderings.

I came by sailboat, a luxury catamaran, with my photographer friend Onne Van der Wal. We were doing an article about sailing the islands for a yachting magazine, but I tired easily of sailing and quickly started thinking about fish. The cat's captain, a tall, goofy Frenchman named Christian, meant to be nothing if not accommodating, but juggling my decayed French and his somewhat pidgin English, I couldn't make him understand the geomorphic features I was seeking, the shape of an ideal sand flat. *Better you listen to me*, was his take on the subject.

"*Io'io*," he said, followed by a French *pfff*, the subtly explosive bubbling of air out from the lower lip. His eyes searched the water, his gaze suggesting that if I would just *look* at the electric blue surface out there, I, too, would understand the patent foolishness of my desires. But I had seen bonefish in the marketplace, smallish specimens hung in bundles by their tails, so I knew they were around. "Nobody catches the *io'io* with the, uh, uh . . . ," Christian waved the back of his hand at the rigged 8-weight Winston XD I held and smiled, "like that. In the nets, maybe . . ."

Christian thought I was a bit of a ninny from the moment I showed him my fly rods. "You cannot catch the *io'io* with that," he decided. He was a charter captain, trained to indulge silly eccentricities—to a point. He wasn't, for instance, about to let me screw up his showing me a nice time.

"Trust me," I argued.

He didn't.

In the southeastern corner of the Rangiroa lagoon, the deep, arterial blue is interrupted by a sudden shelf of sand rising abruptly into shallows that fill the curve of the atoll. At its edge the shelf is a cobbled yellow green, electrified by brilliant sunlight charging the shallow water with an almost photovoltaic energy. Ridges of brick-pink sand rise from the water, long, thin fingers composed of finely crushed coral. The sand slips back into shallow basins and flats that separate it from the rim of the atoll, a half mile away.

Christian ran the dinghy up onto a wide ridge of pink sand, provoking a colony of terns to rise from their nests, screaming outrage and wheeling through the sky. From the sailboat as we approached, I had watched a school of fish sliding from the blue depths up onto the flat, scouring out a run parallel to the shelf and then dropping back off. I had hoped these were bones, but, closer now, I could see they were jacks.

While Christian motored back to the yacht, and Onne wandered off to make pictures, I threw a cast at the jacks off to my left, though they were already zipping past again. Cruising toward me from the right, I spotted a different shape, a pair of lighter, longer shadows. About sixty feet of my line lay in the water. I knew that trying to rip the line from the water and back flip the fly in front of the new fish would be sloppy, but I did it anyway. Both fish pivoted and attacked. I lifted my rod tip and felt the surge as line sluiced through the fingertips of my left hand—bonefish.

The bone shot straight for the shelf. All around, small blacktip reef sharks, which had before seemed lazy, dark forms commingling among the rays and jacks, leaped into action, twitching and charging. I put little pressure on the bone, leaving it enough line to convince the sharks that, whatever distress it might be in, it could still outstreak them in a tail chase. Each shark abandoned its charge after only a few yards, but the bone covered so much ground that it shot by several. Its speed somehow ratcheted up with each new encounter, showering spray higher up the line.

When the bonefish slowed to a cruising speed, the sharks apparently did not distinguish panic and they left it alone. Then, however, I put pressure on the fish, and the bone ignited across the vast fields of ionized seawater. It went like this for some time until I was able to walk the fish up into more shallow water, away from the sharks, and land it. Lifted from the water into the flash-bright sunlight, the bone was a square-shouldered bullet coated with a platinum sheen. The brilliant sunlight played holographic tricks down its flanks.

I moved around the ridges of pink sand, along a channel cut into the acres of back basin. The bonefish patrolled in small groups, a pair here, ten or a dozen there. At one point, I spied a squad of fish moving from the flats through a dip into a deeper basin. I had been working the basin, and I stripped to retrieve enough line to cast, but the line wouldn't come. Instead it flew from my fingers. I had apparently not seen the vanguard of this group, which had already made the basin. One of them launched away with my fly, sending my line singing through the water.

This was nothing like fancy fishing in the Caribbean. I had never changed my twenty-pound tippet—rigged for jacks that would try to part my line on the sharp eyelets of coral formations—or my Abel Anchovies, but the bones didn't blink. Even when my casts fell far short, the fish wheeled and charged.

As I moved away from ridges of the pink and into the wide flats just behind them, the sharks dissipated. Here the bonefish fought only me, and their resistance came in longer, more directed surges. The fish took much longer to subdue, facing only one vector of danger, but I felt better about releasing them into trouble-free water afterward. I felt better for myself, too. Not only did I worry about rogue reef sharks slashing up to take fingers while I bent over to handle a fish, but Christian had warned me that big lemon sharks frequent the pink sands, and that they always seemed to sneak up from behind you.

And, I was alone on the flats. Christian had taken the dinghy back to the big boat, still in sight but out of shouting range. Just how out there I was rang with sudden clarity when, as I stood hip-deep casting back to the rim of a slight depression, the water behind me ripped open like the sound of a giant strip of Velcro tearing. A school of mullet shot airborne—big mullet startled by something much bigger. My stomach ambushed my Adam's apple, and before I knew what I was doing, I learned that my flight-or-fight reflex was oiled, running on all cylinders and leaning toward flight—although within moments I was asking myself just where the hell I thought I was fleeing to. If a lemon shark was tooling around looking for a knee joint to gnaw on, there was no way I could make dry land before it found mine.

I slowed, deciding not to splash around so much, and waded with an attempt at dignity in the face of full-body flutters to a spot within closer reach of the raised sand ridges. I was suddenly keenly aware that, in a place like this, mortality is an immediate topic. This end of Rangiroa is a true wilderness. The day I spent on its flats could have been in 1804 or 1589; with allowance for a little geomorphology nothing would have been appreciably different.

All around me on three sides ranged miles of basin and flat, the work of wind and sea. Beyond ran the low rim of green and, through its gaps, the reef and the open ocean. From outside, surf exploded on the reef, building momentary monuments of spray high into the sky. Maybe I was the only man to fish these flats all year. Maybe I was the first fly fisherman ever to cast here. Maybe not, but the isolation and purity of place allowed that illusion to survive. With my rod arced against the immensity of sky and my line slicing through the sparkling electrolyte spray, joined to the trajectory of a sprinting bonefish, I felt for a moment a part of that wildness.

The next day I flew to Moorea, west of Tahiti, in the Society Islands and received a fax: *Call your brother's house immediately. Very important news.*

Twenty-four hours later, my father met me at the airport in Phoenix. Doctors at the Mayo Clinic had found a tumor they were calling softball-sized on the liver of my younger and only brother, Chris. Because he suffered from Fanconi anemia, his body did not manufacture platelets in significant enough numbers to clot his blood. The surgeons felt that excising the tumor would entail taking as much as 80 percent of his liver. They felt he would bleed to death if they tried that. When I'd left Tahiti, no surgeon on staff was willing to take the chance.

But by the time I touched down at Sky Harbor International Airport in Phoenix, a cocksure doc had stepped forward and agreed to give it a shot. He made no promises but felt like there wasn't much to lose. Without surgery, Chris would die within days. I got to spend one evening with my brother in his bedroom in a small, tidy condominium in Scottsdale. He was visibly sick, pale but shot through with yellow. Anybody could see he was near the end. I combed my brain for right things to say, as if by coming up with some magic word bundles I might somehow make him not have a tumor on his liver. I tried to rally him, tried to get him to think about times when he was young and strong. I reminded him of his days of athleticism and grace, before his anemia caught up with him, when he was the fastest kid on the football field. "Maybe when you're going into surgery tomorrow, when things are getting tough and scary, maybe you can try to remember how it felt when you took a sweep pitch, and you made it to the corner, and you knew you had everybody beat and everything in front of you was just green grass and open field," I said. "Maybe you can just remember that feeling."

"Pretty sad," Chris said, "When my last moments of glory were in sixth grade."

That just made me feel awful, so I sat and talked about mundane things, how my sister liked her new home in Colorado Springs, how the Penn State football team was doing that fall, what we were ordering for dinner. He wanted to discuss only concrete details of the world within the immediacy of the present.

The next day in the pre-op prep room, nobody wanted to say good-bye, but we all said good luck. We all told him we loved him. They wheeled his bed away and we collapsed—me literally, stretching out on the floor of an unused waiting room, exhausted. I passed out. When I woke six hours later, Chris was still alive and out of surgery. I spent two months in Phoenix, helping him recover. My mother and I rented a condo in his development. We cooked and cleaned and played Risk with him. We took turns standing out on his balcony, swallowing from gallon bottles of V8 citrus juices and huffing cigarettes in the dazzling desert heat. And life started again.

Eighteen months later, Chris endured another major surgery to remove another substantial liver tumor. Next the cancer became diffuse, dozens of small nodes littering the swampy architecture of his liver. Radio wave ablation—a wire slid into his body to blast malignant mutant cells point-blank with high-frequency radio waves—worked for a year, but then his body rejected the infusion of donor platelets that helped his blood clot. Once he became platelet refractory, he was down to one last chance.

I was puttering around my house in Montana the day my brother called and said, "I want to ask you something, but you can't answer right now."

Chris called me almost every day—or I called him—and typically the conversation kicked off with some inane pronouncement or another. "I mean it," he said. "You have to think about it for at least twenty-four hours."

"OK," I said.

"I want to know if you'll give me half of your liver," he said.

I thought about it for as long as it took me to hear it, before I said, "Yes."

"You're supposed to think about it," Chris said. "This is serious. It could be serious for you."

"I'll tell you yes again tomorrow, if you want me to," I said, "but it's not even a question."

Because his liver was shot, Chris needed a new one. Because he had Fanconi anemia, he would not be a candidate for the standard cadaver donor program. He needed a volunteer living donor: me. Your liver regenerates. The docs could lop off half of mine, tuck it in Chris, hook up the plumbing and after both of us sat around drinking our meals through straws for a few months, we'd theoretically both be fully functional again. But, because Chris's bone marrow didn't make platelets and his body no longer accepted donor platelets, he would first need a bone marrow transplant to withstand the surgery and, hopefully, annihilate the Fanconi anemia's effects in his own marrow. Our younger sister, Sarah, volunteered for that.

Chris went into Children's Hospital in Boston in late November of 1999 to prepare for his bone marrow transplant. The morning he entered the hospital, he called me from his hotel room. I was still in Montana, would fly the next day, Thanksgiving, to be with him.

"I'm going over there," he said, referring to the hospital, "to start a new life."

"A new life?" I asked.

"One way or another, today is the beginning of a new life for all of us," Chris said.

The century was a blink away from closing. The nation was only weeks away from either partying like a Prince song or facing the Apocalypse, depending on your predilection. The Nittany Lions were stringing together an impressive series of victories. Fall had ravaged New England's foliage, leaving the city brown and stark, hunched against the coming winter. Thanksgiving was an anxiety-addled affair at a Ronald McDonald-like house for families of young people going through organ transplants.

On November 30, a large bore needle was jammed into my sister's hipbone and raw, purplish bone marrow welled up through it. From a bag on an IV stand next to his bed, that marrow dribbled into Chris's immunity-suppressed body. All went according to plan until the third day after the marrow transplant. A small organism called *Pseudomonas*, something that breeds in the guts of most people and is kept in check by ordinary immune functioning, cut loose and bloomed wildly in Chris. He developed mucositis, a condition in which the mucous membranes surrounding his organs and lining his nose and mouth began to disintegrate. He coughed up bloody lumps of his esophagus. He was literally falling apart from the inside out, and soon the process became more than he could endure.

In the early hours of December 6, my brother decided to forego another hit from the morphine pump in order to make a critical decision. His doctors had proposed intubating and sedating him in the hopes they could keep his body functions stable while we waited for his body to accept Sarah's marrow and begin producing white blood cells to fight the infections now dissolving his body. With my parents and me in the room, Chris listened to their pitch. He seemed to comprehend the very high probability that, once he went under, he might never come back.

I don't think I did comprehend that, not like he did. I just saw an untenable misery and death by bloody lumps in the way things were going. Chris sent the doctors out and asked us each individually what we thought. Then he decided to proceed with the intubation.

My brother did not like to be touched when he was sick, when his body was festooned with IV tubes and chest leads. He felt, all through his life, that his flesh had betrayed him. But after he decided on intubation, my mother asked if we could hug him, and he said we could. When my turn came, I wrapped my arms around him. His whole body trembled. I realized he was terrified, and that sent a bolt of fear through me. I held on to him as loosely as I could and said just into his ear, "Promise me that when this is all over, no matter what happens, you'll come and see me."

"I will," he said.

My mother and father said some things to him, told him they loved him. The intubation team rushed in and wheeled him away, down to the ER. My parents followed. I couldn't get

up. I felt pressed to the chair by a weight I could neither lo-
cate nor oppose. I sat in the empty room, staring at the glar-
ing space where the bed and my brother had been, and held
my head in my hands. I had never seen a more frightened
person than Chris when they trundled him off. His teeth had
chattered. It sickened me that my brother should spend his
last waking moments so wracked with fear, and soon my grief
disgorged from me in choking sobs. I felt an arm around my
shoulder, one of Chris's doctors.

"Is there anything I can do to help?" she asked.

"I want to know that we made the right decision," I said.

"You did," she said. "To let it go on the other way would
have been brutal and cruel."

Chris began third spacing on December 15. That's what
they called it—third spacing. A normal human body holds flu-
ids in one of two places—in the veins, arteries, and capillar-
ies of the circulatory system, or in the spaces within each cell
wall. Third spacing happens when fluid begins to fill the in-
terstitial space outside of veins, between cells.

Chris never woke up. He died the next day, December 16,
1999, at the age of thirty-three.

A year later, in January of 2001, I went again to the Tuamotus. It felt like time to get back out in the world, and the
colors of that place, once you see them, are a stain on your
brain: brick-orange fingers of sand rising from the shattered
panes of blue on the flats; pink foam on breakers; a
mahimahi's flanks, the mottled green of brightly oxidized
copper, yellow like mustard plugged in, blue spots like splattered watercolors with darker blue dropped in. They had
crept into my mind intermittently ever since my first time

there. I fell upon the then boyfriend (now husband) of a friend, who with his brothers runs fishing excursions to far-flung places. "Let's go check this place out," I suggested. "Maybe your clients would like it." If he thought so, I figured, maybe I could step back into the guiding business, guide his clients. There were, after all, only so many magazines that would pick up the airfare for me to fly down there. This might, I thought, be a way for me to travel to the Tuamotus affordably and with some regularity.

Dan bit, and I put together a voyage that might let us check out the fishery's potential. The Tuamotus encompass seventy-six islands. We were hoping to see three, maybe four of them. Through an acquaintance I made on my first visit, we enlisted a man named Philippe who fished commercially with handlines for tuna and harpooned mahimahis. We flew to a Tuamotu atoll called Fakarava; at thirty-five miles long by fifteen miles wide just a shade smaller than Rangiroa's lagoon. Philippe met us at the airstrip, along with every child on the island. He didn't know anything about bonefish, certainly not where to catch them in shallow water. Hardly anybody did, it seemed, prompting Dan to observe, "If they don't eat it, and it doesn't kill them, the natives rarely know much about it."

"We see the *io'io* in the passes, in October or early November," Phillippe said. "Maybe spawning."

Philippe did know a thing or two about tuna, and once we'd settled in, he fired up his thirty-five-foot *bonitier*, a wood-hulled motorboat popular in French Polynesia, and steered us through a gap in the fringing reef in the island's southeastern pass. The atolls of the Tuamotus form round bathtubs of warm shallows in a far deeper ocean. Although tides are not strong here, at low tide the water inside the lagoon is pulled through—in the case of Fakarava—one of two narrow passes, a process which churns up tremendous currents. Tuna, jacks, mahimahis, and large sharks gather outside the passes on outgoing tides, waiting for the buffet to be flushed their way.

In the deep blue water, birds hovered over the surface and dolphins raced the boat. We saw tuna leaping, blasting through the surface, their archipelago of yellow caudal fins flashing in the sun. Phillippe began rigging buoys. He chunked a bonito and threaded a hook into its head. The hook was attached to one-thousand-pound test line, which Philippe used to wrap the head to a stone. He made several wraps around the stone, slipped another hunk of bonito onto the stone, then wrapped more. The line was attached to a buoy that had been painted green on top, orange on the bottom. With a slipknot, Phillippe fastened the line to the top of the buoy, too, so it rode upside down in the water, orange up. Then he dropped the whole collection overboard. The stone sunk, unraveling from the line, freeing chunks of bait as it descended to form a vertical chum line.

Tuna traveling at any depth would find one of the baits and follow the scent to the others, eventually winding up at the hook. When a fish tugged, it untied the slipknot on the buoy, allowing it to flip right-side up. When Phillippe saw green riding high, he drove the boat over to the buoy, snagged it with a boat hook, and began hand over handing forty- or fifty-pound yellowfin on board. We caught four tuna as fast as we could haul them aboard, and that was enough for Phillippe. Back on shore, he made a sauce of garlic, lime, vinegar, salt, and pepper, and while the day's heat subsided, we sat in the sea breezes and sank our teeth into forearm-sized hanks of sashimi.

For the next two days, Phillippe motored us around the lagoon. We checked out flats in the high-sun middle of the day, oblivious to tidal charts, paying little attention to bottom structure. We didn't see much and started talking about cutting our losses. Instead we snorkeled, became bedazzled by the buck-toothed parrot fish in their metallic greens and blue, by a lagoon floor clotted with coral brains, then falling away to a blue so rich as to have its own texture. Streams of light raced under the waves. We watched schools of fish pour before us like a glittery, viscous liquid flowing through another liquid. A patch of finely spotted orange-brown something extruded into a moray eel as thick as my calf, its knotty head leading flanks so fluid it seemed as if the animal were mostly made of water.

Snorkeling in the passes, whisked along by the current on the incoming tides, we saw "sleeping sharks," the white-tip lagoon sharks, far below us—miles down it seemed, peaceful and graceful and silent. Everywhere we snorkeled we saw dozens of sharks: blacktip reef sharks, whitetip reef sharks, lagoon sharks. From above, they all seemed harmless until occasionally a shark drifted up in the water column, eye-balling us, sizzling our nerves a bit.

One day Phillippe stayed home and his brothers, Rito and Jean-Louis, took us to the northwest corner of the lagoon, to a place where wide flats subsumed to shaggy coral heads. The lagoon shoreline stretched in a long, empty arc beneath galleries of bowed palm trees. A huge bent triangle of pink sand jutted into deeper water, flanked by extensive flats for miles on either side. Right away we saw bonefish, four or five, all singles. They all followed our flies, then spooked.

We walked a long way, seeing hundreds of fish, but catching only a few. A storm bullied the horizon and hurried us back to the boat. But like so many tropical storms, this one was on its way elsewhere, which left us sitting on the boat, frying surgeonfish Rito had speared for us. We poured buckets of fresh water over our heads for showers. In the sky, light from the lowering sun bounced into canyons of cloud, painting relief with palette-knife strokes of only pink and white. Dan's shortwave radio picked up a station playing "Jambalaya" in French, and some other songs in Tahitian.

Rito played the spoons and we all sang the songs we knew or the choruses we could pick up. After dark, Orion appeared briefly overhead before the moon, nearly full, dimmed the stars, lit thin puffs of cloud around the sky, and cast a splintered white path across the sea's surface. Later I unrolled a sleeping bag on deck and listened to the hiss of the water where it boiled over coral heads. It felt very good to be right there, if for no other reason than "right there" was so far away from everything that had gone before it.

We tried other places, motored away for overnight explorations of the other side of the lagoon. But this spot, Teha-Tae (pronounced *cha-tair*), drew us back over and again. We saw enormous bonefish, and caught a couple of them, but mainly stood around with puzzled looks after each refusal. Now that we'd found them, neither Dan nor I had the hang of what we needed to do to make these fish eat. Still, I was feeling like this was a place with rich potential, and I liked being here. It had a feeling.

One day I wandered alone along the farthest reaches of the Teha-Tae flat and for no obvious reason I started thinking about Christmas, just the month before. My family had gone to

Colorado Springs, to my sister's house. My brother had died so close to Christmas the previous year, and we had all spent so much time and money traveling to and from Boston that we hadn't gathered for those holidays. There hadn't been much to celebrate. The following spring, my sister had become pregnant with her first child, the first grandchild in the family, and there did seem a reason to celebrate. We started looking forward to the Christmas of 2000, made plans to spend it at her house, expecting her to be expectant with eighth months of pregnancy.

Except before that could happen, on November 16, she delivered prematurely—at twenty-two weeks, far too prematurely for anything to be done about it. The baby was born alive and died in her arms, eleven months to the day after Chris had died.

I don't know why, walking the Teha-Tae flats, hunting for bonefish, I thought about that most recent holiday, but I did. I remembered how sad we all were, but how nobody said so. We were just trying to put together some sort of Christmas. I tried to imagine my family as viewed by someone peeking through the windows, and I concluded that we were just . . . sad. And then I started thinking about Chris and how much I missed him and how hard all this was, and before I knew how it happened I was bawling. Not just crying, but—all by myself, remote, far from other ears and eyes—I was suddenly wailing in the Tuamotu wind, and the sadness blew into every part of me. I walked and wailed, feeling so tired of letting go of things.

And then I saw a big bonefish gliding through the shallows, unraveling a lacy wake behind it. Still crying with an energy that made coordinated motion barely possible, I made a shaky, almost angry cast, and a futile little strip. The fish took. It was the biggest bonefish I'd hooked in my life, and it made three or four long runs deep into my backing. I was still hiccupping and sniveling snot, but I worked the rod as the fish headed for the deeper blue and a coral ridge I could see there. While I had him in the open field with twenty-pound test, I levered some muscle. When I dragged the fish near and could see his shadow in the waves, I became . . . not happy, really, but amazed. It was a huge bone, so big I couldn't tail it. I had to press the fish against my leg and roll it up my thigh to pluck the hook from its mouth.

Now I was confused, torn from visceral grief only moments before to this inescapable, if untimely, notion that something had happened and now I felt a little better. I did feel better, too. Not *better* better, not *hot damn* better, but I didn't want to wail anymore. For a moment I thought I should do some communing with the fish, but then that seemed profoundly stupid. We'd had our moment together, and anyway, there was no bond between that fish and me. The bond was between me and this place. The fish was only an emissary, sent to remind me. He took off slowly, pale blue going darkness as he burrowed into deeper water.

The next winter, 2002, Dan and I brought clients on an exploratory trip. After two weeks of guiding from the same catamaran I had first come to the Tuamotus aboard, we made our last foray to Rangiroa's pink sands. The rotation worked out so I had a day off. Dan dropped me off at the finger ridges that I had come to years before, where I had caught my first South Pacific bone. The water was almost dead flat in the shallows. Outside the reef, through gaps in the palm trees, breakers hurled spumes of foam into the air.

I fished without much gusto for a while, caught a few nice bonefish. Clusters of high, pearlescent clouds towered around the sky like cities in the distance. Higher in the glare the pre-historic silhouettes of great frigate birds skewed the sense of time. I waded back to the pink sands and a fairy tern followed me, hovering no more than a few feet over my head, the edges of its wings lit with a porcelain hint of translucence. A stroke of faint blue reflected on the curve of the tern's breast. I could see its black pellet eyes, focused on the water in front of me. The bird was expecting something.

I climbed up onto the ridge of pink sand. Six years had gone by since I first came to this place. Back then I was one year out of Menninger and trying to find an entry back into my life, searching for a dialectic or a bonefish, whichever hit me first. I left here to find news of my brother's cancer. Now, without thinking of what I was doing, I started scraping big letters in the sand with my foot. I gouged out the words, "Chris Hull lives."

When I was finished, I looked at it and felt sad for my brother, and for the me who was so thrilled to be here six years before, blissfully unaware that Chris had just received his diagnosis and eventual death sentence. The man who was here back then had the depression ward behind him and a new world before him, fresh points of view, any one of which could be brand new stories. Things could have turned out so many different ways, but in two more days he was going to learn that, of course, they couldn't. I did not feel like I had come full circle. I felt only like it was hard to understand how to know so much sadness and still wobble along.

Later that evening I sat alone on the trampoline between the catamaran's bows and watched night gather over the sea.

A tern rose from the dark blue of the evening water. It lifted over the horizon into a bank of white clouds, their undersides powdered purple. The bird held its wings above its head, then was lifted, tilted by the breeze, whisked to one side. It dropped back down against the background of water, where I lost track of it. I wanted for the tern to rise again, but it didn't. It was gone so quickly.

The moon rose, illuminating ragged and complicated bas-relief cloudscapes outside the lagoon. Stars trailed behind them like the footprints of time. The only way to distinguish the night horizon from the sea was to notice a more fluid shimmer in the reflection of the stars. I didn't know that, after this trip, I would not return to the Tuamotus again. I just knew that I had found a place I hadn't previously guessed existed, and that it wasn't a place where everyday details felt loaded with memory and sadness. I saw something brand new every day here. Nor was it a paradise where everything was all better, where I could disconnect the tendrils that wrapped me to a time before this one. In these immense pools contained by porous, seemingly insignificant rings of land, I had found a third space all my own.

While I lay back on the trampoline waiting for sleep, water pushed against the bow beneath me. I felt the tropical night temperature on my skin, just warm enough to let me know I was different from the air.

Knots

SOME KNOTS YOU TIE and others tie themselves. The former attach you to a probative process, fix the backing to the line, fasten your line to the leader and the leader to the tippet, join your fly to a gossamer length of tippet, and connect you to a foray into the world of water. How many times do you react to a strike, then pull your line in to see the wisps of a former knot still curling the remnants of the cleaved tippet? The value of knots escalates in direct proportion to the size of the fish, until, in the salt water, solemn attention to the wraps and loops you tie approaches religion. How the knot tightens matters. The fact is, sloppy knots usually break, and sometimes break your heart. They're endemic to the chances you'll never have again.

Fishing knots can be admired the way sailors gaze upon the elegance of rigging. I can have a wondrous experience just watching the loops of a blood knot slowly sliding together to become wraps and, finally, reach fixity. At the moment of that final tug, I'm ready. It's time to start looking around.

Think of the names alone: the nail knot, the blood knot, the clinch knot, the clinched half blood knot, the blood bight knot, surgeon's loops, spider hitches, the double turtle, the Palomar, Arbor, Albright, Gray's, Duncan, Crawford, Brubaker, Huffnagle, the King Sling, the Berkley Braid, and my all-time dance-hall favorite, the Bimini Twist. Those names suggest an enticing diversity of purpose, though the truth is, at the core of it they're all doing the same thing—just holding on (you hope).

We only need to know a few, as long as we tie them well. We need three or four knots for freshwater fishing, a couple or three more for the salt. Still I find myself from time to time wondering about a new knot, thinking about learning something different. For these I like to turn first to knot diagrams, those fantastic expressions of useless compassion—the artistic gestures of people who *want* to help but just didn't really think it through. Occasionally you see one that you can actually follow—the simple mapping of a blood knot, say—and even these bear an iconic disregard for reality. But I love looking at them. They're so hopeful. They're spirited as a Chamber of Commerce Fourth of July parade banner in a dying little town.

Knots have always inspired hope. At one point in time an entire school of thought, promoted by Lord Kelvin, of temperature fame, posited that the world could be explained by knots. Kelvin thought the smallest particles of matter were actually vortex loops consisting of different chemical elements, each containing unique knotted configurations. The

universe could, according to Kelvin, be understood by ana-
lyzing the knots that entangled elements in the universe's
ethers—which is why Kelvin's name blesses a temperature
scale that nobody uses, and Einstein is on all the posters.

Atomic theory shit-canned Kelvin's knot thinking, but did
nothing to knock down the significance of knots in human
history. The oldest known pierced-object pendants (which im-
plies cordage to thread through the piercing), a wolf tooth
and a flaked bone point, date from three hundred thousand
years, implying that knot tying is one of the oldest forms of
applied geometry. The oldest knot survives from 7200 BC,
part of the Antrea net, a willow bark fishing net recovered
from a peat bog and now on display in the National Museum
of Finland in Helsinki. The knots making up that net remain
in common usage today.

The ability to knot cordage allowed primitive man to
weave fishing nets but also to wrap stone spear points to
wooden shafts, fasten ax heads to handles, lash vegetation for
shelter, sew together pelts for clothing. The roles of virtually
all of the shiny fastening devices you see in bins in the hard-
ware section of Home Depot were historically filled by
cordage, which required knots. In lieu of writing, the Incas
used a knot-tying system called quipu to account for and
store massive amounts of information—the color of the cord,
type of knot, and its position on the cord all conveyed units of
meaning in recording the contents of warehouses, population
figures, and taxpayer accounts. In Europe, knots became
gauges of both depth and speed. Knots are now analyzed in
the study of weather (knotted orbits) and genetics (knotted
DNA). And knot theory remains a happening slice of modern
mathematics, but math . . . we'll get to math later.

It's surely true that knots made and continue to make fishing possible. Without them, fishing would be called, as it is, sadly, in many Southeast Asian countries, "blasting." Knots allow us to deliver our lure far deeper into the distance than we could carry it by hand. Oddly enough, the very things we assume are holding things together are precisely where our best efforts are likely to fall apart. A knot reduces the breaking strength of the material it's tied in by 25 to 50 percent, a drawback we all have to accept.

It's the knots that tie themselves that everybody sees as a plague, a pox on the house of fly fishing. But they're unavoidable. Even the truly great fishermen cast knots in their lines from time to time. The difference is the great ones call these "wind knots," disentangling themselves from culpability. Blaming the wind and getting away with it is one of those clever joys fishermen get to know about as they grow into things. Even tip wraps—the beginnings of knots wrapping themselves around solid objects—seem like the spawn of forces outside of ourselves. I remember losing a hefty tarpon once and finding myself explaining it the same way I remember my friend Dodd explaining the loss, on another outing, of a well-hooked sailfish: "Got tip wrapped." I got tip wrapped. Not, I stupidly dipped my rod tip and wrapped the line around it. As if the tip wrap had been imposed upon us by some implacable force, which left us not at all responsible for the screwup.

I think the funniest knot I've ever seen was one in my friend Mark's line. It should be said that Mark and I spiced our fishing with a certain . . . oh, we saw it, I think, as teasing. I've subsequently been told that we were so cutthroat and competitive that we impinged on other people's enjoyment, which is really too bad. There was, admittedly, one-upmanship in those outings.

Which is not to say we weren't looking out for each other. When Mark moved from Montana to Manhattan, and I happened to be visiting the East Coast and had the opportunity to fish for stripers with Dodd, I told Mark to jump on the train and come on up. Mark is one of the most athletically gifted men I've ever met. Only his diminutive stature prevented him from become a famous athlete—that and an absolute lack of desire to become a famous athlete. He picked up everything quickly, which was unfortunate for him, because one of the things he picked up quickly was gelande jumping, a numbskull endeavor in which one uses regular, fixed-heel downhill skis to pretend one is a Nordic ski jumper. What happened to Mark happens, I suppose, to all gelande jumpers at one time or another, only more so to Mark. His father, a physician, who happened to be watching from a seat halfway up a chairlift at the moment of Mark's fateful flight, later said that, after the initial impact, Mark looked like a starfish pinwheeling down the slope. Mark wound up with several fractured vertebrae and one of those arresting cocktail-party explanations for why his neck is so stiff.

When we went striper fishing, Mark was swearing he was all healed up, though I had trepidations—made more acute when Mark showed up with felt-soled wading boots as his footwear. We fished from Dodd's dory, which provided a fiberglass surface to stand on. Ever see saltwater-saturated felt on wet fiberglass? It's like Wile E. Coyote trying to get off the highway after he's oiled it to catch the Road Runner.

Mark had never fly-fished in the salt before, never caught a striper, and we were all anxious for him to get one. Fishers

Island Sound was flat and vaporous, one of those warm summer days in New England when the ocean sways around all glassy and smooth, as if it had never thrown a fit in its life. The bulges of stripers chasing bait bloomed all over the surface and we had Mark throwing poppers to make things interesting. Line management was always one of Mark's weaknesses, and on this day, it wasn't long before, while lifting his line to cast his popper again, he noticed that, in all his staggering around to keep his wet-footed balance, he had created a sprawling knot in the line he'd stripped in. The knot was not about to slide back out through the guides. The popper dropped in the ocean a few yards from the boat.

"Great," Mark said, turning his attention to this knot, which, being in the fly line itself, could not just be snipped off. "This is when I hook the fish."

So he did. While Mark dug and pinched and twisted and tugged, a bluefish spotted his stationary popper floating right beside us, ripped the popper from the surface, and hooked itself. At first the knot—which, under Mark's careful ministrations, had added several loops and grown to about the size of his head—would not pass through the big stripping guide closest to the reel. Well, no, at first, Mark fell down in the boat. Had he not, only six months earlier, broken his back, I would have found this uproariously funny. As it was, I had to wait until I knew he was OK to see the humor, though then it came clear fast. He held his rod up, even while sitting on his butt in the bottom of the boat. While the knot and the guide imposed upon each other an impasse, Mark's rod tip U-ed toward the water. Then: *sproing!* The knot sucked itself in enough to squeeze through the guide, line shot out, the rod tip bounced back to straight—and the knot hit the next guide and jammed.

By now Mark was back on his feet and already threatening to go down again. He held his rod high and the pressure on his line bent the tip right back toward the handle. The bluefish seemed determined to head straight down. Then another *sproing!* as the knot squeezed through the next guide. Mark regained some footing, but little composure. He saw what was happening, the knot pinching through each guide, then adhering to the next one, the rod tip springing straight, then hauling down. The knot squashed through another guide, and we all saw it headed for his tip top. Mark had no idea what to do differently.

Neither did Dodd and I, so we stuck with what we had already been doing to contribute, which was laughing really hard. The knot hit the tip top like it was tearing off beer caps with its teeth. The rod pretzeled down again, but the tip top held. The line vibrated with tension. Mark looked at us and grinned foolishly. The line shot through. Mark fell down again. But he eventually brought that fish to the boat—or at least close enough that we could handline it the rest of the way in.

I've knotted line in grass, trees, and shrubs, knotted line around my fingers, around my ankles, and around my neck. I've had knots in my reel that required complete disassembly. I have, in the past, just quit, walked right off the river over a knot, seeing it as a portent, or a totem of the day to come. I used to hate knots that tied themselves in my line. I saw them as intent thwarted, time poorly wasted, and the perfect symbolic logic for frustration. The greater the spaghetti ball, the more thoroughly twisted and snarled my sense of frazzle. Trying to force things always makes it worse, though sometimes a quick flip of the wrist is just the ticket.

And then one day, a frigid February afternoon on Rock Creek, I held an eagle's nest of monofilament to the low, cold winter light and saw in it a thing of beauty all its own. How the movement of my wrist and hand through space had created an interweaving at such remove, all the way at the end of my line, beguiled me. I held the knot up to the light, watching as a cold frost began to scale its surface, and caught the reflection from the sun as I examined the shape of the structure and the frozen curvilinear motion of my knot.

I sat on a bench of snow covering a downed cottonwood trunk and, with fingers as cold as lead pipes, began to unravel the mystery. I was fascinated by the space between loops of line and how they could influence my next tug. It seemed as beautiful to know that no line occupied these spaces as it did to see how they shaped the whole. I knew it would be quicker and easier to snip and retie, that even if I untangled the puzzle I might well end up cutting away kinked and ruined monofilament. But I wanted to know how I had done this. There was something in that still display of tensile strength and in the memory of the fly line gripping itself. Unwinding a knot is one of the few instances in which we can actually see memory happening backward.

It's the same process by which we learn to read water. To a novice a river is a huge gush of current, a salt flat, just an empty stretch of chop. Once you spend some time fly-fishing, rivers start to come apart. Flats fall to pieces. You learn to follow rivulets of current and swirls of eddy, discern shadow from depth, pick the one push of wave moving out of sync. You learn to judge by what is apparent—the current readable on the surface—what might be happening below the surface—which is a little like reading literature, or being a parent. If you pay enough attention, let yourself feel patience, knots come undone.

There was a time when I experienced my whole existence as a slow-tightening knot. It felt like coils of life backing over each other and tangling, then slicing into their own surfaces a little as they gripped and refused to back off. I've done a lot of work to loosen some of those coils, and these days generally try to keep my line straight. At least, when I feel a little wind knot, I don't keep casting.

But I do wonder how we—the royal we, the grander scale—find ourselves in this slow wrapping, this strangling process we seem unable to extricate ourselves from. I can see out my window how Big Sky country is becoming Big Roof country. I do understand people's desire to live in the fabulous West—I moved here from somewhere else myself. I made sure, though, to pick a house that was already standing, rather than building a monument to myself. I instantly started on a wetlands restoration project. I'm not feeling terrifically self-righteous about it; I *am* part of the problem. But I'm willing to be thoughtful about my role, consider my actions and ways that I can ease some of the pressure.

Because at a certain point there are tangible realities. At a certain point must come some recognition that we as a collective lose more than several individuals gain when the rivers run thick with septic runoff and empty of trout, when the landscape is clotted with T1-11 and Tyvek logos, and when the wildlife is reduced to whitetail deer and starlings. Snarled traffic now backs up on the bridge over my river for hours every day. How did that happen in Montana?

There are simply certain phenomena that free-trade, free-market, free-for-all economic theory does not respond to efficiently. The ruination of beautiful places springs right to mind. We've been brought up believing some withering lies in this country. One of the most awful is that there are no limits to what we can have. It's just not true. Montana, the West, is as good an example as the Gulf Coast used to be. Everybody wants a piece of This. But everybody can't have a piece of This, because This is intangible. Despite our best attempts to package it, This resists commodification. When the Madison valley, or the Upper Blackfoot—or any lovely place still hanging out on the fringes of wildness—becomes chockablock with four-bedroom homes perched on the riverbanks, and fertilized, pest-free lawns stretch to the riparian zone, when lanes and cul-de-sacs loop around and roads wind over feeder streams and under the shade of cottonwoods and back on themselves along the way to a knurl of Wal-Marts and Targets and Golden Arches clogging the earth with concrete, let's face it: this is no longer This. Nobody has a piece of it anymore.

So how do we untie this tangle? First we need to see it for what it is, start picking threads, tugging on them gently. I'm not short of answers. Build up, not out. Accept the regulation of subdivisions. Embrace zoning. Demand stream setbacks. Abandon the equally dogmatic and ridiculous notion that a house is not a home until it's graced with a handsome patch of freshly clipped, pest- and dandelion-free Kentucky bluegrass right outside the front door. There are other answers, too, ones that demand mass introspection, a change in the way people actually look at the knot, which is much harder work. These answers lie like the core of the messiest of knots—easy to spot but difficult to get started on: live within who we are. Release ourselves from expectations. Stop trying to close the gaps in our lives by filling space. Accept a social responsibility. Believe that what we see around us is true.

Once you've been outside the northern boundary of Yellowstone Park and seen Slough Creek's broad sweep of meadow stepping up to benches of trembling aspen, lit golden by September sun, how can you not believe the truth of that place? Once you bump into two subadult grizzly bears on the flanks of the granite-peaked Mission Mountains, their silver-tipped pelts glowing like a full-bodied halo, you know everything you need to know about what should happen in that place.

It's true all over the world. Watch the prehistoric shape of a five-foot-long tarpon, bucket-sized mouth agape, water pouring from its scales like champagne as it leaps into the sky behind a school of mullet under the blazing Florida sun. Then ask yourself: does this place need another beach villa?

We have to start picking at that core of gnarled, wrapped, and knotted filament. Those of us who care have to take the argument away from defensive short-term thinkers, tangled in their own high-blown ideology, and start talking out loud about other possibilities. One of the first acts of responsibility is to see clearly. We've got to talk about what is obvious. We've got to pull the first loop free, see where that leaves us, and what the next move might be. Maybe then we can discover that the emptiness in our lives is a great place to live. Maybe we can begin to feel an unclenching of something that has wrapped itself, without our even realizing it, around our hearts.

Estancia del Zorro

NEVER BEEN FISHED.

Nearly every fisherman I talked to in Chilean Patagonia spoke of streams that had *never been fished*. The concept didn't seem unusual to any of them. A man in Coyhaique asked me if I knew any Americans potentially interested in investing in a lodge operation. He wanted to offer spike camps to fish rivers that didn't even have *names* yet.

Two weeks after fishing in Chile's vast, unpeopled regions of Patagonia, I spoke on the phone with Jay Burgin, the American ownership partner of Estancia del Zorro and Cinco Rios lodges near Coyhaique. "Just since you've been down there we've found another spring creek," Burgin said. "It's never been fished that anybody knows. Not with a worm, a fly, or dynamite caps. The guides went up into it and say there are thirty-inch fish living there."

And, even though these are fishermen talking here, I believe it.

I believe it because I fished at the tiny sprig of spring creek that winds through Burgin's Estancia del Zorro property, and heard stories of a legendary fish nicknamed "Tippet Cutter" that lived under a bridge. I fished with 2X tippet—2X on a spring creek—in anticipation of the rodeo that would break out if I were to hook something like the thirty-two-inch, fifteen-pounder that came out of the creek a couple seasons ago.

But mainly I believe it because Rodrigo says it's so, and I've come to believe everything Rodrigo says.

I told Rodrigo I would kiss him, which probably weighed on him a fair bit. He was the guide, after all, had to make the gringo happy, but he's a Latin guy, and so was probably bugged about the prospect. Who knows what gringos are going to insist on following through about? Well, I only told him that because two days before I had fished the Zorro spring creek and caught tons of decent fish, just pop, pop, pop, one right after another—in my first five casts I'd caught three fish—but nothing particularly hefty. And today I wanted something . . . hefty.

I was trying to be reasonable. I'd heard over and over about the ten-, twelve-, fifteen-pound browns lurking under the cutbanks. "Rodrigo," I wanted to know, "how could a fish that big hide from me in this tiny little creek?"

"Those dudes are hard to catch. They are wild and intelligent," Rodrigo said, "That's why they are big."

Still, I wasn't demanding one of those hook-jawed savages. I just wanted to catch something that felt . . . hefty.

Twenty-three inches, I decided arbitrarily. Rodrigo was going on about fish as big as my leg. "We catch a twenty-three-inch fish and I'll give you a kiss," I had said to him.

The wind was blowing so damned hard I honestly doubted I'd be able to throw my fly into the water, let alone present it in any way that might trigger the lizard brain of a smart fish. So the statement seemed like a safe way to awaken Rodrigo to my desires without committing either of us to anything life altering. And my very sexy and beautiful girlfriend, Ronni, was standing just down the bank snapping photos, so I didn't think I was creating unreasonable expectations.

Look, I meant, *I don't think I'm going to do too well today, but if I do, boy will I be excited!*

You can't write about fishing for a living and not realize that you're always in danger of braying. So I know it would be wrong to suggest that fishing at the Estancia del Zorro spring creek is too easy. After all, one does not fold oneself into the matchbox seats of a modern airliner and girdle half the globe in search of a place where the fishing is just sort of marginal.

The Zorro spring creek winds in near figure-eight S curves through broad pampas. The land here opens and rolls like the lower Madison valley—bunchgrass flats and deep, scrubby ravines, forested benches with rimrock upper lips—only greener, fuzzier, and more lush. The first pool I approached with Rodrigo was the same one I'd approached first with Dave Bloom two days earlier. With Dave I'd taken a fine sixteen-inch brown on a Taylor's Fat Albert beetle here. Dave had told me that the creek bottom was crawling with *pancora*, a boxy little cross between a crab and a crayfish that he referred to as "the building blocks of giant trout in South America." Rodrigo thought I should dispense with the niceties of dry-fly fishing, slap on a Nere Nuff Whitlock sculpin, and dredge subsurface without ceremony. "We could fish with beetles, but big trout are very smart," Rodrigo said. "They know there are not many beetles right now."

I think Dave probably knew this too, but had patiently endured my dabbling with dries. At any rate, I was already believing most everything Rodrigo said because he'd spent his whole life fishing in this area, starting as a boy wrapping monofilament around a coffee can.

One thing I love about Jay Burgin is that he's giving guys like Rodrigo the opportunity to share their local knowledge. It'd be easy enough for Burgin to pack his two Chilean lodges with Sage-totin' guides for hire on snowbird hiatus from Montana and Alaska. I understand, too, that some folks, when they go fishing in far-flung places, want their guide to serve sandwiches with mayonnaise and American cheese, be conversant in American stock prices, and elocute in American English at least as well as the Bush twins. Me, if I go to Chile to fish, I want to learn a little about Chile—beyond the flourishing wine selection—while I'm in the midst of it.

So Burgin's program of educating Chileans through an apprentice program and training them in the finer points of American fish guiding is, to my thinking, a fine thing for all involved, particularly us end users. And I appreciated it more sincerely every time Rodrigo spoke about his country. He talked of love gone wrong and fabulous adventures. He told me that his father was thrown in jail twice for not getting home by dark during the infamous curfews of the dictatorship—a chilling reminder that, even in this isolated outpost, Pinochet's gruesome grasp was never far away.

These are pieces of Chile only a local can give you. When we see a small, black bird with a red back, a *negrito*, Rodrigo tells us that it's colloquially called the *colegial*—the student—because of its red backpack. He calls the goofy Andean lapwings "hangry birds" because, "When you get close by they make a lot of noise, like they're hangry."

I did scoff a bit at Rodrigo when we approached that first bend of creek again and he pointed to the little spot where he thought I should drop my fly in the pool. Actually I didn't scoff so much as I laughed and laughed. The wind was blowing so hard, seven out of ten casts hit the pasture rather than the stream. But eventually I plinked one in place, and a flash came off the bank and made my rod dip like a dowser's. The brown was nineteen inches long, more silvery than its butter-bellied North American cousins, its flanks less crowded with spots.

Chile is a country that without apology sold its economic soul to Milton Freidman during the Pinochet regime. Chile is so pro-free trade, a fruit industry spokesperson told me, that it has its own IRS—an Instant Ratification Syndrome, that is— which causes the government to ratify every trade agreement dropped in its lap before bothering even to check how the document squares with Chile's own domestic laws and regulations. I was talking to people like fruit industry spokesmen because I was in Chile to lead the journalism portion of a course being co-taught through the University of Montana's journalism and law schools. We were examining the impacts of the free trade agreement Chile had signed with the United States twelve months before.

What we learned is that Chile is a country whose export model is seen by some as the star of South America in terms of economic stability and the production of wealth, but also a country that suffers from the ninth worst income distribution gap in the world (right up there with other "stars" like Nicaragua and war-torn Sierra Leone), a country that enjoys a blistering 6 percent annual GDP growth *and* continually expanding unemployment, and one that is rapidly and eagerly transforming large portions of itself into a place that looks just like the stretch of highway between L.A. and La Jolla.

Patagonia is a pleasant exception. Patagonia is what it is—and what it is is magnificent, wonderful, *fantastico*, and laced with fishful rivers—primarily because there are no roads into the region. Only in relatively recent years has there been regular air service. Stockaded along the eastern frontier by the looming volcanic peaks of the Andes, hemmed by fjords on the west, sliced by the Straits of Magellan to the south, and isolated from northern population centers by hundreds of miles of roadless mountain terrain, Patagonia is an inner kingdom little disturbed by the busy machinations of the export wizards in Santiago.

Except, of course, for the timber trade, in which multinational bandits like Trillium and Boise Cascade scalp vast swaths of ancient and rare Patagonian forest, exporting raw logs in exchange for silt-choked rivers, and compromised ecosystems, albeit far from the pesky scrutiny of U.S. conservation groups. Or the mining industry, in which firms like Noranda propose building five dams on magnificent rivers to power a new aluminum smelter—far removed from bothersome air and water quality standards of the developed world. Or the aquaculture industry, which provides consumers in

Dallas and Pittsburgh with plump salmon fillets but spares them notice of the toxic chemicals poured into Patagonia's fjords, or the degradation of already depleted wild ocean stocks, five pounds of which are used to produce one pound of farmed salmon.

But ecotourism, there's an export sector the fly fisherman can line up behind. Fly fishing in Patagonia is the region's biggest ecotourism activity, and growing fast. According to an Austral University of Chile researcher, three years ago 60 percent of fishermen in Patagonia were Chilean, and about 30 percent came from the United States. (The European Union, Canada, Australia, and New Zealand sent most of the remaining 10 percent.) According to the most recent available figures, in the next year, 2002–03, Chileans accounted for only 38 percent of fishing days, while Americans claimed almost 48 percent.

Still, anglers log only about fifteen hundred fishing days in northern Patagonia annually—by comparison, Montana racks up about three million angler days. Chilean Patagonia is a big, empty place. Fly fisherman have been poking around Chile for fifty years now, and we've only scratched the surface. Folks are just getting around to many of the springs and smaller streams.

When you go to big-name lodges in Argentina to fish, you might spend a whole week on one river. On Estancia del Zorro, the spring creek was but one of many angling options. The Rio Pedregoso (which means "many rocks" and quite accurately describes the gravel-chocked, freestone stream) offers five or six miles of wade fishing, before dumping into the Coyhaique, a productive, floatable river. Across the Argentina border, the Estancia offers access to another spring creek, as well as miles of the walkable Rio Mayo—plus the second, newly discovered spring creek, which is a tributary to the Mayo. Burgin's Cinco Rios lodge, near Coyhaique, boasts float fishing, jet-boat access to the far reaches of several rivers rich in trout, small-stream wade fishing, lakes—essentially enough varied adventures to color your dreams for weeks.

Rodrigo and I moved up another bend in the creek. The wind bored into my body through my pores. Rodrigo pointed out a little seam he thought I should cast to. I laughed and bonked the back of my head with the lead-eyed sculpin. But as soon as I put the fly in the water, I hooked, struggled with, and quickly landed a twenty-one-inch brown.

"Close to a kiss fish," I told Rodrigo.

"Maybe we should quit," he said. "Go over to Argentina."

We didn't, and around the next bend the stream opened in a long, straight run. Current bounced off a shelf and sliced out the left bank in a slight divot. There was a seam about two feet wide sheltering a back eddy flush against the bank.

"Cast in there," Rodrigo said.

I laughed. He was serious.

Eventually I made the cast. The water's surface bulged as a trout rushed to my fly. This was a very nice fish, and it raced all around the narrow sluice of stream in front of me. It burst upstream and wrapped itself several times around the roots of some overhanging plant, then commenced to leap into the air and splash back into the water. Again. And again. Four times.

I realized that on such a short leash—the fish wrapped leader, not line, around the roots—all that leaping would mean a clean break pretty quickly, and I had suddenly become emotionally attached to this rather hefty fish. I tossed Rodrigo the rod and plunged into the creek, provoking more leaping from the fish. I yanked my line free of the tangle and then wrangled the trout. It was easily over twenty-three inches long. Rodrigo looked at me.

"Let's go to Argentina," I said.

So we did. We drove fifteen minutes up the gravel road past a highland swamp upon which sailed black-necked swans and upland geese. Black-faced ibis stalked the marshy shallows. The spring creek wound through these wetlands and came out the other side, channelized again. We saw its elegant scribble reaching far across the pampas. "We are wanting to explore that," Rodrigo said, about some more *never-been-fished* waters in the distance.

We passed through Chile's and then Argentina's border crossings. Argentina seemed even more windswept and desolate, but ten minutes later, at a nondescript wooden gate, we turned onto the Estancia Numancia and drove a long dirt lane through clots of sheep. A body of water opened to our right and we saw, seemingly floating above the surface of the lake, the puffy pink bodies and question-mark necks of flamingoes. Thousands of coots and ducks dotted the water's surface. We approached a wooden bridge, transparent from missing so many planks. Rodrigo gave us the option of exiting the vehicle before he drove over it.

"The bridge will hold us, I know," he said, "but if you don't want to try . . ."

It held. We drove a bit farther and, though there was little evidence that a stream wound through the windswept grasslands ahead of us, we stopped and walked overland about thirty meters. The stream opened its course beneath us. About twice as wide as the Zorro spring, it worked through deeply gouged cutbanks and beds of aquatic weed.

Whereas all the trout on the Zorro creek were browns, this Argentine spring held exclusively chrome-flanked rainbows, which attacked my fly with fervent recklessness. The rainbows don't grow as large in this creek as the browns across the border—both Burgin and Rodrigo told me they've found some fish well into the twenties, but nothing gigantic. What they might have lacked in size, however, the Argentine rainbows overcompensated for in ballistics. Few casts failed to turn fish, and few fish failed to launch an air show once they came tight on the line. Too easy, really, except you wouldn't come all this way for just sort of marginal.

On the short drive back across the border, I kept my eyes in the sky, looking for Andean condors, which congregate in this area.

"Listen, Rodrigo," I said, "about that kiss stuff . . . maybe we'll work on that the next time I come to Chile."

"Don't look for me," he said.

That settled, we drove along contentedly. Rodrigo spoke of his family and his dreams. "What I want to do is get a pilot's license, fly helicopters," he said. "We have a bunch of lakes . . . they're full of big salmon and trout and nobody can get to them."

Never been fished.

Saint Juice

YOU'RE NOT REALLY TRYING to catch fish when you take a young and exuberant male Labrador retriever fishing. You might as well start up a lawnmower, strap it to your belt, and drag it on into the river with you. If the dog is not in the water scaring fish, he's roaming the bank, following sniff trails, maybe one that leads to something as fabulous and luxurious as a deliquescent dead fish. By then you're quite rapt in your casting form, or in the tricky way the river's current is spooling off a rock, or the way in which a tiny insect humming above the water's surface is going to invoke heartfelt commitment from a stupid little trout. Meanwhile, the dog, having arrived at the putrefying corpse of the aforementioned dead fish, has a decision to make: eat or roll.

I've seen Juice do both. I've scooped my fingers well down his throat to dislodge the spiny remains of hammer-handle pike on the mudflats surrounding warmwater ponds. I've also seen him come trotting along the riverbank after an extended absence, his black snout slashed with what could only be a canine smile, his pelt coated with a latherlike white slime that was once an intact, if rapidly decaying, sucker that someone tossed on the riverbank.

Juice has never been consistent about it, rolling or eating, never exhibited a solid preference. He likes to keep his options open. On the one hand, Juice hates being clean. It's like he's being made to wear a dress. On the other hand, rotten fish tastes . . . well, who knows why Juice tilts his nose at one dead fish and finds himself unable to overcome its gustatory appeal—or why he inhales the bouquet of another and thinks: *this goes so nicely with what I'm wearing today.* If choice defines character, Juice is dodgy at best. He has his good days and his bad days. He's a dog like the rest of us.

Juice is a male black Lab. He is a tremendously handsome and well-muscled Lab, and I'm not the only one who thinks so. His sire was a show dog, his mother a field trialer. Juice has a classic, blocky head with a bit of seal-like roundness to his skullcap. He has lovely reddish-brown eyes. His chest is beamy and his hips slim. Alas, he spent his formative years getting by on his looks.

I'll let you know up front that Juice is not lying at my feet as I compose this ode to him—my office is upstairs and he can't make the climb anymore—but he's still kicking. I wanted to write about him before he died to avoid obituary, those sad odes to passed pets that always make me well up (if you want to read a great one, check out Tom Junod's elegy to his mastiff "Marco Died" in the July 2002 issue of

Esquire). It hasn't been easy. Juice has taken a lot of shots at dying.

There was a period when Juice's youthful urges were simply too much to quell, and he strayed. I don't mean only that he roamed wherever impulse took him, though he did that. I mean that whenever I tried to establish the bounds of acceptable behavior, I found his muddy footprints all over and far outside those bounds. In his younger, more exuberant days, Juice was in such a hurry to check out the world that he dogtrotted on a skew, his rear end angling to overcome his front. My friend Dan Bennett, who spent as much time with Juice as any of my friends, took a look at the dog trotting toward us one day and said, "Your dog's out of alignment. He needs his paws rotated."

Juice has gone through phases. For a while he was the dog about which good friends like Dan said, "You're not bringing your dog, are you?" Then he was the dog about which good friends said, "Hey, don't bring your dog." Now, as if they've recently swapped out their brains, these same people ask, "Where's Juicy?"

The first time I took Juice fishing he was only a few months old, a bundle of puppy breath and fluff and needle teeth that ruined everything they came into contact with. This was on the Blackfoot River, downstream from where one of the major tributaries enters. There's a high bank across the water, and I remember distinctly looking at the clay bank pocked with swallow nest holes, black holes in the yellow-brown wall, beneath a stripe of late-afternoon blue sky. Along the bank stretched a run of some obvious depth. It was a late-August day and as the sky deepened caddis began swarming the river's surface.

Juice was a small but handsome puppy, confident about his place in the world (at my feet, or at least very close by). He had not yet been for his first swim, so when I waded in, he expressed an alert sense of alarm. But when he saw I wasn't going very far, he relaxed and sat on the cobbles, then started licking stonefly casings from them, then chewed sticks. I caught a few trout, but eventually I decided that the best drifts would be tight against the opposite bank. I started wading toward them. That's when the shrieking began.

When I heard the sound, a visceral screaming that sounded like an animal being skinned alive, I whirled, expecting to see a small black puppy dangling from the talons of an eagle or an owl. But there was no raptor attacking Juice. Rather it was a sudden change of heart about his place in the world—momentarily alone and vulnerable. He sat on the cobbles at the water's edge, nose pointed at me, and howled the most pitiful racket. I wanted to make it stop for a number of reasons. One was that I worried some nearby angler or camper at the campground upstream might think I was inflicting cruelty on my dog. Another was that, although a predator had not inspired the outcry, these pathetic warblings might inspire a predator—whereas I'd never given them much thought in terms of personal safety, coyotes, mountain lions, and bears were suddenly a concern.

I grieved at the place in my heart those hideous chords struck. What kind of guy could let a puppy suffer such obvious anguish. Then again, there were trout on the opposite bank. And don't young dogs, I wondered, need to learn self-sufficiency? So I turned toward the pocked clay bank and the strip of blue sky. I tried making the long reach cast. I got a drift or maybe two down before I gave in to the howls. If I was the kind of guy who learned from experience, I might have seized this early opportunity to understand something about how the emotional whims of a dog could influence my day. I had more opportunities as time passed and Juice discovered his ability to run faster than me, which allowed him to visit every angler up and down the horizon. You can imagine the joy most people felt when a ninety-five-pound Labrador came crashing through the river to stuff a snout in their crotch and inquire about the availability of treats.

At least once before I finally broke him of—or he got bored with—that habit, I had the opportunity to use it to my advantage. I was wade fishing on the Bighorn River. What happens these days on the Bighorn is that a dog doesn't have to run very far to bug the next fisherman, so I had Juice tied in the shade of a tree on the bank. I caught two, maybe three long, shiny rainbows on some emerger the size of a diatom before anglers began converging on me from both directions. I thought: *you've got to be kidding me*. But they waded right into my run.

"What are you catching them on?" one man called to me. Generally, I'm not a zero-sum guy; I don't fear that every fish someone else catches is one I won't. I'll happily share successful patterns with people—but not when they've barged right into my casting range and started whipping away.

The Bighorn where I was fishing is like a big spring creek, flat with shiny, lazy curlicues of run and eddy. A successful presentation includes stealthy casting and long drifts in uninterrupted current. I knew exactly how to deal with the interlopers crowding me from both sides. I waded to the bank and pretended to switch out my fly. The interlopers used this opportunity to squeeze in even closer to the patch of current

I had been fishing. So I unclipped Juice's leash from his collar. Within moments he was lunging through the silent stream, plowing splash and spray as he furrowed through the river to visit the new folks.

"Hey, call your dog!" one of them yelled.

I shrugged, shook my head and said, "Damn Labs."

Juice learned about fishing though, and it transformed him. Once he understood that every so often my waving arms would drag something alive through the water toward him, Juice, for at least a narrow majority of his fifteen years, stood chest-deep in the water by my side and stared at every cast I made. When I pulled a fish in, he would wade deeper, maybe even swim around, wanting to look at it. After only the first couple of encounters, he wasn't interested in trying to pick them up in his mouth. He just wanted to watch them dart around and shimmy. He always reminded me of a little boy watching fireworks—utterly occupied, wholly beguiled.

On my boat, an inflatable raft, he was much the same. He'd clamber over the rowing frame—and anybody's unguarded open beers—to watch a fish being brought in. When the action was slow, Juice climbed up onto the side of the raft and lay there, head dipped over the side, nose inches from the water's surface, staring intently at every new piece of minutia the river brought to him. He remained captivated for hours. I knew we'd entered the downward slope of Juice's life when one day he fell asleep staring at the river. I noticed him going slack, and sliding toward the water. This was followed by a sound somewhat like *Sploosh!* and the whites of Juice's surprised eyes disappearing in the plunge cylinder as he went completely under.

⌘

When I first started writing about Juice, over fifteen years ago, this was going to be a different story. At the time, I was thinking I was going to train him to obedient perfection, then field trial him until we won something big. He had a great nose, and a huge engine. I'd teach him discipline and teamwork, and away we'd go. Then I'd write about the field trial circuit, the empty miles between events, the lonely nights in hotel rooms with my dog. I had already, without attending a single event, formed the opinion that I would not like field trials, that I would find them fraught with politics and jealousies like so many other silly contests people pitch themselves into—league volleyball, tournament bridge, fishing tournaments, writing workshops. I imagined a noxious minority of hypercompetitive monomaniacs brandishing seditious rule interpretations. I have no idea if any of this is true because I still have never attended a field trialing event. What I learned fairly early on was that training Juice for field trials was a matter of potential versus imagination. While I do still think Juice had the instincts to potentially be a trial champion, I realize I don't. I don't have the patience or the endurance, nor do I have the wits to know when to back off and let the dog be the dog.

In the field, what happened with Juice and me was probably inevitable. Juice is a flusher and a retriever. I never expected him to quarter over open ground, pivot on his nose, and button birds down until I could get to them. I expected him to plow through heavy cover and scare the bejesus out of roosters and sharptails so that they would forget I was around and fly. I expected him to fetch up the remains. It was, I thought, not too much to ask.

Instead, I became highly educated about just how fast, sprinting in heavy boots through coulee bottoms and the ankle-rolling corduroy of plowed grain fields, one has to move to stay within shotgun range of a galloping dog. I became educated in how to swear while breathing heavily. I learned the fine calculus of how, based on the area beneath the arc where birds busted into the distant sky, to judge how far ahead of me my unseen dog ran.

Even during the years of his best behavior—which I guess really means two or three of his later years, those involving diminished physical capabilities, but predating his realization that he was too old for discipline—in the field Juice would get drunk on bird scent and lose his inhibitions. He'd get ideas. I didn't mind as long as he did that in my vicinity. I liked it best when he hung around within shotgun range. It's a sort of détente we spent a long time trying to reach. I tried letting him run behind the truck the last half mile or so to the field, trying to burn the stink out of him. I tied fifty feet of heavy climbing rope to his collar and let him drag it through the coulees to slow him up. Still, nobody ever called me and said, "Hey, let's take that dog of yours hunting."

Like many Labs, Juice liked to please his people, but not enough to make a practice of it. It always seemed like a happy accident to him when something he'd done—a long, fine retrieve or well-timed halt when a skunk waddled out of the brush—earned lavish praise. He'd sit on his haunches, tongue lolling, head tilted up slightly, ears flattened so that his eyes squinted a bit, wearing an expression that suggested, *Hey, this is all right.*

⌘

There are sixty-five million dogs,[1] kept as pets in this country, and most of those are kept by people who think their dogs
are special. Probably, they are. Anybody who denies that dogs
have distinct personalities hasn't spent enough time around
dogs—and I'm not referring to some anthropomorphic projec-
tion of our own personalities upon our pets. Given an exposure to a certain number of dogs—assuming the exposure
does not come in, say, your role as a lab hand about to shoot
toxic chemicals into the dogs' eyes for medical testing, or fire
bullets into their haunches, an old military technique for
training medics—it becomes quite apparent that dogs are
each unique bundles of niceties and neuroses. What com-
monsense argument could possibly suggest they're not? If
dogs do not think, if they possess no imagination, no ability
to conjure and connect image and meaning, then why do they
dream? Why bother?

Supposedly Great Thinkers like René Descartes posited
dogs were merely machines, that howls of pain they emitted
when provoked were the equivalent of clanging cogs in an un-
greased gear. This sort of logic prompted biologist Claude
Bernard to perform a litany of appalling in vivo experiments
on dogs in the name of science. Look, the Supposedly Great
Thinkers asserted, these howls and shrieks are not expressions of pain, but rather adaptive responses that dogs have
learned will win our sympathy.

I continually fail to understand why the wails of dogs are
adaptive responses while the same noises made by, say,
Christians nailed to crosses means something far more significant. Why are we so afraid to release the sovereignty of

1. http://www.hsus.org/pets/issues_affecting_our_pets/pet_overpopulation_and_owner-
ship_statistics/us_pet_ownership_statistics.html

sentience? Why insist that nothing in the world around us has a soul? Because then souls and sentience would have values beyond the ability of our possession-grubbing selfishness to possess? I guess it's a lot easier to justify much of what we do if we can believe that everything we find is meant solely for us to take.

I'm certain Juice has a soul, and that it's sleepy. There was a time when I thought Juice was possessed of a high intellect, as well. Then I got Sola, a female yellow (almost pure white) Lab, and learned what actually smart dogs are like. I've had friends tell me they thought Juice was a deep thinker—still waters, and all that. More than one friend described him as a Buddha. If this was true, my wife, Ronni, has suggested, it might explain a lot about why Juice never seems to listen to us: he's occupied practicing mindful meditation. Certainly there have been times when I've wondered what kind of thoughts were rinsing through the brain encased in his handsome black head. So often he wears the expression of someone who's just found something he wasn't even looking for.

He is not simply interested in sustenance and comfort, though, unless you consider goose shit sustaining. I know this when we're driving in the truck and Juice thrusts his head out the window as if wherever we're going, he wants to get there first. I know he's thinking about what's next. I see his ears fluttering in the wind like bat wings, his tongue flapping against his jowls, I watch his nose twitch, his eyes work through changes—there's something going on there that has nothing to do with food or comfort. He's anticipating. He may not know what, but at those moments, he's full of wonder.

Dogs test the core of our humanity. Our relationship with them contains enormous potential for abuse. They put up with so much. It's all incumbent upon us to treat them well. At the same time, we could learn a thing or two. Dogs don't want much. They don't want a Sony PlayStation, a Stumpjumper, the new Mercedes SUV. Dogs want to run when their legs get the itch. They want to know where it's OK to relieve themselves. They want to be fed. Put in some solid sleep time. Dig a little. They want now and then to be told they're wonderful—or at least that you're not furious with them. Maybe a scratch behind the ears, maybe a rump rub.

My dogs want to chase certain birds and swim in the creek on hot days. Occasionally they want to roll in a dead fish. Tell me where in that list is the bad? Sure, dogs eat the garbage, chew the sofa, shred your cross-trainers, piddle on the floor. Still they're so much nicer than teenagers. How many profoundly disaffected dogs do you know?

Loyalty is the attribute most often pasted on dogs. I'm always surprised when I hear people using that against them, swinging the term like a battle-ax. They say, How could anybody admire a creature so blindly, stupidly loyal? It's, of course, far more complicated than that. When Juice and I were charged by a cow elk outside of Glacier Park, do you think my dog made a loyal effort to defend me?

We had been fishing the North Fork of the Flathead River and were beginning our walk across the broad floodplain back to the truck when the cow materialized before us. She must have had a calf secreted in the brush somewhere. I'd never been attacked by an elk, but this one didn't hesitate more than a moment before dropping her head and charging. Juice took off as fast as his scrambling butt could scoot him across the riverbed moraine, dodging in and around the willow and cottonwood scrub. Where did he run? Along what vector did he drag this pursuing peril? Right to me. And once he zoomed past me, he spared not one backward glance to assess how the elk's flailing hooves might impact my flesh. He ran to the river and leaped into it. The elk abandoned the chase only after steaming up and down the bank a few times, veering between the paddling dog and the terrified idiot brandishing a piece of driftwood. Juice simply swam away from all the uproar. Where's the stupid loyalty in that? What dogs have is faith, and it's a better brand than we practice.

It's funny to me, the parallel evolutions in our approaches to life (I mean mine and Juice's). My dog, in his younger years, was nearly frantic in his attempts to sniff, taste, immerse himself in everything lying before him. He nearly ran over himself—or, when leashed, tugged his collar through his neck—in his eagerness to inspect every new dog on the landscape. He pissed all over his legs in his haste to finish marking one bit of territory and scurry along to douse the next spot. If Juice could really control everything he staked out with spritzes of urine, he—and I, by extension, as his owner—would own most of Missoula. Now Juice lets other dogs come to him. Now, when a new scent arrives on his palate, he will stand in one spot and sniff every angle for five, ten minutes at a time, sucking every bit of olfactory information from it. He squats to pee.

These days a walk with Juice is a slow affair. He hobbles on stiff hind legs and breathes in decibels. I try to walk as slowly as he does. Sola is good about staying close, so I don't worry about her. I try to stay with Juice, make him feel like he's not being rushed. He almost always falls behind anyway, only now he doesn't care. Going slowly gives him more time to eat snow and gobble goose poop. He knows the lane. He knows I'm going to go down it, and then come back up. Now, he knows, I'll find him.

Stephen Holbrook Jackson, who I doubt ever had a dog, once said, "Man is a dog's idea of what God should be." Well, I mean . . . what crap. Of course, Holbrook Jackson was a literary critic, and they're famous for straining to pass loosely formed bits of intellect.

Who knows what dogs see in us? Dogs look to us for daily food and the handout of treats. They need us to recognize and treat their ailments. They want to ride in our cars. They prod us to scratch their ears. Only in the pathological world of the Religious Right would an individual turn to a god for such an array of purposes.

Then consider the cruelty—both casual and vicious—so many dogs are treated with. According to the Humane Society of the United States, of the thousands of cases of animal cruelty reported in this country annually, 70 percent of the victims are dogs. The abuses recorded in 2003 included throwing, drowning, suffocating, dragging (as in behind a car), stabbing, burning, the very macho practice of dogfighting, and animal sexual abuse.

Those are merely a few of the individual crimes; in this country we still tacitly endorse the institutional abuse of dogs and other animals. In 2004, the year of the most recent figures available, the U.S. Department of Agriculture conducted experiments on over 64,000 dogs.[2] One organization estimates that the total number of animals subjected to brutal experiments in the United States annually is over 20

2. http://www.hsus.org/animals_in_research/general_information_on_animal_research/

million, a significant portion of which are dogs[3] (see http://
www.all-creatures.org/saen/fact-anex-jul03.html). Dogs are
blinded, burned, shocked, deprived of food and water, exposed
to radiation, sizzled by caustic chemicals, poisoned, addicted
to drugs, and driven mad in severe confinement—in the
name of science, yes, but also in a far more shameful name:
money making.

Then there's plain old neglect—dogs left without food or
water, without proper veterinary care. And then there's the
three to four million cats and dogs euthanized every year[4]
just because they're in the way—unplanned, unwanted, un-
cared for.

Does any of that sound godlike? So to critic Holbrook's
nonsensical observation, I would offer writer Ed Abbey with a
twist: When man is dog's best friend, dogs have a problem.[5]

Despite all this, I do think Juice likes me. He's often so
aloof it's hard to tell. He's an alpha male, and has that alpha
stoicism—he's neutered, but he doesn't seem to think so. In
our everyday life, Juice couldn't care less if I'm immediately
around. Unlike Sola who always wants to be near The People,
Juice spends most of his day dozing on a couch in a room far
from my sight. Still, I'm the one he waddles over to and flops
in front of when he wants a butt scratching. It's certainly not
a worshipful relationship, but there's at least the sense that
we're in this together.

My feelings toward him are equally complex. I thought
Juice was the cutest thing on four paws when he first ambled
into my life. I played with him, letting him chew me with his
puppy teeth until my forearms bled. Later, a battle of wills
evolved. I hated that the dog was so beyond the bounds of my
control. His impudence pecked at my patience, and I made

3. http://www.all-creatures.org/saen/fact-anex-jul03.html
4. http://www.hsus.org/pets/issues_affecting_our_pets/pet_overpopulation_and_owner-
ship_statistics/hsus_pet_ownership_estimates.html
5. Abbey said "when a man's best friend is his dog, that dog has a problem."

the mistake of construing his behavior as a challenge to me. It poked right into some of my rotten spots and on occasion I found myself driven to blind rages. I am ashamed to admit that I sometimes—long ago and in another time of my life, but *I*—unleashed these frustrations on Juice physically, in the shortcut, symbolic logic that angry men so stupidly resort to. I hit the dog. Not corrective taps, either. On a few occasions, I took it out on him.

I hated myself afterward. I never once struck Sola, and remain convinced that the only way to earn Juice's undivided attention during the Wild Years was a swift controlled swat to the haunches. But those were controlled swats, not meant to inflict pain or fear, and I sometimes went further. What I hated was the loss of composure, the surrender to frustration. The shortcut. Worse is the fact I let it happen with an animal that I knew would take it.

There's no reason to hit a fifteen-year-old dog, not even correctively, and yet still, sometimes, I find myself feeling like it's just what I want to do. When he's eating dirt or deer shit that I know he'll regurgitate later on the carpet, when I'm rushed and he won't curtail his olfactory inspections to hurry along with me, Juice has a way of pushing himself right up against the limits of my patience. I feel it bubbling up from deep in my blood like a black, boiling surge. I can always stop it now, have been able to for many years, but I don't even like to feel its simmerings. It reminds me of too much that was out of control in my life.

Last winter I made a startling realization while walking down the driveway, watching Juice eat snow. I love winter, love the blue evening light in which I walk the dogs the quarter mile down our drive to the mailbox. Juice loves winter, too, becomes more visibly alive, more rambunctious in the cold. He loves to roll in the cold white powder, and he loves to eat snow. I wouldn't care, except he usually comes into the house after a big snow chow and vomits a pool of liquid heavy on viscosity. So I endeavor to stop Juice from eating too much snow. I'll point at him and wave my hand, make my "no" face. He knows what I'm telling him.

He watches me checking his snow eating, and gauges the distance between us. If he feels I can't close it quickly enough, he'll snatch another mouthful. It's a daily passion play. Until one evening last winter, as I rushed forward to scold him for chomping another snoutful, I stopped, flush with the understanding that Juice is just being Juice. These were *my* limits I felt pushed against, not his, and my limits were mainly arbitrary. In fact, there was no real reason my limits couldn't be withdrawn miles farther into the distance. I was the one who, at that moment, felt the surge of tense anger, the sick anxiety that followed. Furthermore, I didn't have to feel it. Juice didn't care. He just wanted to try a little more snow.

And then I realized what a gift Juice gives me. He will keep being himself, and he will keep giving me opportunities to alter the way I act. No matter how many times I act badly, he'll give me another chance. He will teach me just how far away from patience I really am, and he will do it without judgment, as if he is some kind of hairy black saint. Saint Juice.

On Good Friday two years ago, Juice raided the closet where I was keeping Easter basket fixings for Ronni. He ate about three pounds of chocolate, and an unhealthy dose of foil wrappers. Chocolate is, of course, toxic to dogs. I found Juice in the throes of convulsion, spewing a slurry of poison from both primary orifices. When I tried to lift him, to get him to the truck and into town to the vet, he was as stiff as a frozen salmon. Juice spent two nights in the emergency vet clinic, a scary punishment for gluttons. His attending vet told me he'd never seen a dog so sick that lived. My friend Dan had a different take. Dan said, "That dog is too dumb to die."

Juice tried to prove Dan wrong when Ronni and I took him on a hike outside of Lewistown, Montana, one hot, dry day the following summer. We hiked a ridgetop where the map suggested we would find some springs. But there was no water. We led Juice to one patch of snow, and gave him our bottled water to keep him chugging along, but when he reached the vehicle at the end of the hike, he collapsed, perilously dehydrated and in some sort of cardiac distress. He was too far gone to drink, so I poured coolers full of water from the trailhead spigot over him. We sped the hour's drive to the nearest vet, a laconic crank who handed Ronni a coffee cup perfumed with booze while he jabbed an IV needle into the dog's foreleg. We decided not to leave Juice overnight there, and took him with us, IV bags dangling from the coat hook in the backseat of the extra cab.

The next brush with death came last spring, when Ronni and I took the dogs on a drive to the Hi-Line along the Canadian border. We stopped along the Milk River not far from Havre. Ronni stopped the car and she and I unloaded some binoculars and water bottles for a stroll to possibly see some spring warblers in the cottonwoods along the river bottom. I looked up to see Juice homing in on what I immediately identified as some sort of spine—an elk spine, I thought. It's not uncommon, in Montana, to find pieces of carcasses scattered around public lands. Hunters leave the parts out to be scavenged, an interesting justification for dumping.

We were two days into a four-day car trip and I didn't really relish the notion of Juice smelling like decomposing elk—because I knew he intended to roll in it—so I jogged over. By the time I reached Juice, the elk spine had changed shape, gathered and coiled into a rattlesnake as long as I am tall and as thick as a fifth of whiskey. Juice's curious snout hovered within three or four feet of the snake. I couldn't step between Juice and the snake to head the dog off, for fear of having rattler fangs perforate my buttocks. Juice was an old dog by this point, weak in the hips, so I grasped his tail and slung him sideways, knocking him down. I reached around from behind, and dragged and lifted ninety-five pounds of baffled Lab away from the snake.

Next came the seizures. We don't know why he gets them—full grand-mal-type convulsions. They last an hour and a half. His body seizes and twitches. His eyes flick back and forth uncontrollably with nystagmus. He loses bowel control. We sit with him, pet him, try to offer comfort. Nobody knows what else to do about it.

After all those dodges, a while back we learned that, saint or no saint, Juice has no claims on immortality. He let us know this by acquiring a load of cancer. After failing to completely remove a malignant mast cell tumor from Juice's chest, my vet told me the dog would probably not live more than a year. That was two and a half years ago.

The fact is, Juice is a fifteen-plus-year-old male Lab, and we have no pretension on his continued longevity. Fifteen years is a long Lab life. Juice is practically a relict. His muzzle is sprinkled white, and snowy hair tufts jut from between his toes. He breathes like a crosscut saw. His hips are so frail he sometimes falls over by himself. He's stone deaf, which I know, because I've stood behind him saying "Go fishing?" or "Birds," or "Popcorn"—I taught him hand signals by pointing and tossing pieces of popcorn to various corners of my living room; he grew obsessively fond of it—or any other of the terms that would normally inspire some sort of antic response, only to watch him continue staring placidly out the window.

Juice is going to die someday sooner rather than later. I have to acknowledge that. Dan doesn't think so. When I told him about struggling to deal with the fact that Juice is near his end, Dan said, "Five years from now we'll be sitting around having this same conversation, and Juice will be snoring on the couch."

Juice still loves to go fishing. He is slow and stiff coming. He slips on the rolling cobbles of the bank. Even a slight current knocks him into the flow. I won't take him to the big water, because in his dotage he's forgotten that he's not the bull of a dog he once was. The last time I took him to fish the small creek that runs through our place, it was early summer and the water was still a bit high. This creek is wadable at almost every point, but not when you're an old, arthritic dog. Juice piled into the current, and I wound up abandoning my casting to rush downstream and steady him as he clung to a partially submerged log. Gone was the profile of a strong, sleek animal at home in the water, slicing through current and using his thick tail as a rudder. In its place was a wet-headed, pop-eyed refugee, struggling to keep his head above water, surprised at the dilemma he suddenly found himself in.

I had to boost him back onto the bank. Then, of course, he tried to do it again, plunged right back in when I waded around to position myself at the next hole. So the fishing was over early, but it was a lovely day for a stroll, brand new cottonwood leaves flittering in the breeze, song sparrows lacing the June sunshine with their sweet, liquid piping.

Here's how Juice and I go fishing now: when I feel like I've been ignoring him too much, I take a rod out the front door and join it up, run the line through the guides. Juice watches, eyes alight, weight shifting slightly on his feet, a whisper of the hot-footed prancing that once marked his impatience. We walk—I walk, and Juice crow-hops—to the pond at the edge of our yard. I stand on the bank and start casting. Often I don't even tie a fly on. There are trout in the pond, big trout now, but I'm not really interested in catching them. Or I'll put it this way and see if it makes sense—focusing on catching fish would distract me from fishing with Juice. So I cast my empty leader at the rise rings. Juice sits as transfixed as ever, watching every cast. From time to time, he'll wade chest-deep, turn and look up at me and whine for more action. But usually he forgets to be upset for long. I turn his attention to a new portion of the pond with a redirected cast, and he's got all new potential to wait on.

I feel that this summer will be the last one Juice and I will stand side by side near the water—but I felt that last summer, and the one before, too. It doesn't matter, now, when the last time the water reflects on his black coat, or the sun lights his soft, rich eyes. He doesn't care about the last fish, or the next one, or whether it's honest of me to take him out there and cast without a fly.

Neither do I. Juice has let me look honestly at the way I've lived with him, and he's never cared that it's not all pretty. It's odd to say this, perhaps, about an animal that drools in his sleep, eats clumps of grass left behind by the lawnmower, and sometimes craps on the carpet, but I think Juice is wandering off toward a state of grace. I'm just glad he's walked me along part of the journey.

Wonder Time

I USED TO DO this all the time. That's what I am thinking: *There was once a time . . .*

I stand beside my truck and hold on with one hand while I finish pulling the waders off my foot with the other. A film of river lies fresh and wet on the waders, and I smell it in the cooling evening air. The rings of trout rises well up and peal away on the surface of the river. A whitetail buck steps to the edge of the meadow and sniffs the mixing breeze. The chirps of crickets are landmarks across fields that fill the darkening space to the west, between the dirt road and the mountains half a mile away.

Mark is waiting beside the passenger door, waiting to get in and go. He wants to get back to town, maybe head to the Rhino bar, maybe drink cold beer from a glass. I want to hesitate and wonder, just to see what will happen. Maybe nothing, but I remember what has happened during this time before. It's enough to hold me a few moments longer.

Shadows, which had been creeping along while the sun was still around, take over and make themselves disappear. I can *see* light leaving the land. This is the time every day when creatures filter from deep cover to feed and drink. During daylight, these are shy animals—grouse, skunks, owls, elk, bears, maybe moose, maybe even a mountain lion. In the dark what you see comes mostly from inside. In these moments in between, nothing is out of the question.

When I used to do this, there was no Mark and no Valley of the Moon. Now I stand beside the truck, and across the pickup bed, Mark knows I am thinking about something, so he says nothing. He lets me linger while night turns the day inside out. Maybe he feels it too. I can only hope, because asking wouldn't work. Mark is part of this by virtue of the fact that he's standing here. He's a friend and we fish together. This evening is early summer, my first summer in Montana. For years I have watched gaudy sunsets splashed on a heaving ocean. Now I am reacquainting myself with sundown in the woods. But the changes I'm experiencing begin in another place, a long time ago. I can almost feel what I felt then, though the fact that I have to find it as memory, of course, means I can't ever really feel it the same way again.

It takes a long time to be over. When I know I've made Mark wait long enough, we get in the truck. On the highway, I see the deepening sky come closer to the earth, ending in black, peaked downslopes, as if its bottom has dropped away and emptiness is there now.

⌘

When I first became aware of twilight in the field, I was with a girl. It's a wonder, really, that I was aware of anything but her. This was way back when, high school. Her name was Sherrie, she had a big nose, and I loved her. Today you could say almost anything you want about it, but those things remain absolutely true—I wasn't very good at love, but I loved Sherrie, and she had a big nose. She was lovely in the way sixteen-year-old girls can be lovely when they're not "cute," although she was as prone as any of them to show up wearing a ponytail sticking out of the side of her head.

In the spring, in the evening, Sherrie and I would drive down to the marshes on Lake Erie in northwestern Ohio where a flat, brown river called Mud Creek emptied into Sandusky Bay. In the fall, I hunted ducks in this marsh with my father. He was friends with the farmers who grew tomatoes for making ketchup and cucumbers for making pickles in the diked-off fields edging the marsh. I became friends with them, too, as much as teenagers can be friends with adults.

I used to drive Sherrie in my dad's station wagon up onto a brush-banked dike. The dike elevated us so that one corner of a harvested cornfield opened like a private theater. Several blocks of corn stalks were always left standing. Across the corner of the field stood groves of naked hardwoods, branches splayed like hands cupping buds of spring growth. Behind the trees swelled fields of cattail, stiff and straight as brushstrokes, and then the wide, silent waters of the bay.

I stopped the station wagon on the dike and we got out. An electric buzz told me the keys were still in the ignition, but the door slam knocked silence into our ears, and from there we climbed up onto the hood of the car. We scooted so we could sit and lean back onto the windshield. Our arms floated around each other and fit as we watched sunset draw a low pink band down into distant tree lines. We'd kiss or not.

Because the earth was so flat, night came as a perfect indigo cap on a dome of cool air, dropping in from above. A deer would step into the corn stubble, then another, and another. We could hear the papery rasps of corn sheaves fiddling against stalks, but not the steps of the deer. Overhead the dome deepened and viscous night poured down along its edges.

Sometimes we would talk about our friends or things that had happened that day, but usually by then we'd had half a dozen conversations already since school let out. Usually this was the time we talked about ourselves. We'd say things we might be afraid to say in front of other people, thoughts we feared might make us weird. Or worse: things we thought or cared about, but that nobody else might think *mattered*.

At some point Sherrie would say, "I love you, boy." I would say, "I love you, girl," and we would both mean it in the simplest, most unfinessed form, a way you can't mean after the first time you say it, a way you may never believe in again. And that would always make us be quiet for a while.

The geese arrived first by voices, cries floating in fragments above us, snatched away by high winds we couldn't even feel. Overhead in the night sky we saw their silhouettes, loose, liquid Vs sailing among the starlight. I lay with her head in the pocket of my shoulder, her hair fine on my cheek, and watched the rafts of geese float through the stars, their honking stronger but still distant. Between flocks we talked about how we would always want this, how we wanted to live where we could hear geese in the evening, how someday we would have a house, together, where geese flew overhead.

So they say time loves a hero . . . but there's nothing intimate there. We so seldom know much about how anything will strike us until long after it already has. Most of us expend a great deal of energy trying not to let our gaze stray beyond the recent shallows to the deeper blue current of the past. One late-October day, after I had lived in Montana for many years, I went to the river, to the same place where Mark and I had fished when I first moved here. I had been sick—just some rundown flu—but this day I was tired of being sick. The sun fell evenly across the fuzzy, blond hillsides and I was certain this afternoon would be the last warm day of autumn, the last real day of dry flies. So I went fishing.

I had been fishing this piece of river all fall, before I got sick, with Mark. He was getting proficient. One night in September he dragged an eighteen-inch rainbow out from under a log, then turned around and pulled an eighteen-inch brown from a riffle farther upstream. But this day Mark was not with me because he had moved away, and I was sure it would be my last outing on this stretch of river until the next spring. In Mark's absence, I was left with Juice and a new Nanci Griffith album, *Late Night, Grand Hotel*. I had bought it and not even listened to it yet, saving it until I drove to the river. She sang a song about the morning, said it was a miracle that came around every day of the year, and I was starting to think I knew what she meant.

Juice I liked being with again. Juice was a sixteen-week-old black Lab at this time, a pure rascal. When you train a young dog, it's important to realize that in the early stages almost anything that goes wrong is your fault—which can be depressing. But I thought we were over that. I thought Juice and I had reached a new high ground in our relationship, one where he knew how to listen consistently and, when he didn't, it was his responsibility.

At the river I pulled off the gravel road and parked on the edge of an empty field. A faint trail led through a rolling meadow of tall yellowing grass. By the time I reached the hole I wanted to fish, the sun had slipped behind the ridge to the west. Across the watercourse a stand of cottonwoods lifted shaggy yellow canopies into the sky. The cottonwood leaves shimmered in the breeze and the rich yellow rippled. The river squeezed into a narrow run, which channeled closer to the opposite bank. On my side lay three large rocks in a flat but roughly isosceles triangle: baseline parallel to the current, apex closest to my bank.

With the direct sunlight gone, I felt the air mix around me, breezes cooled by the stream swirling through the day's remnant warmth. Overhead the sky had deepened into royal blue, and the bone-white wispy clouds had their bottoms burned hot orange. Quickly enough the orange would spend, the white on top would fade, and the clouds would bleed rose into the evening sky. But at the moment that I noticed, the colors of the sky and autumn cottonwoods flickered on the stream's surface like the history of flame. I had just enough time.

The browns were spawning, but I fished dries, figuring that fish still hungry enough to rise weren't serious about their sex just yet. I worked my slot, starting at the top and moving downstream, then casting back up. Juice chewed a stick at my feet, noticing every now and then that I had moved, getting up to trot to me. When I had worked down and was almost all the way back to the top of the slot, I cast and caught a bulge in the current and my fly rode its dome. I could distinctly see my fly, a Pale Evening Dun, floating dragless, and for a moment that seemed all that mattered—a fly borne on a dome of current, colored by autumn. Next came a subtle strike, graceful and slow as a dolphin rolling. Just before the fish broke the surface I caught the movement, then heard the tiny accent in the rhythmic tinkling of the current, and saw a flash of bronze rolling away. I struck back.

I didn't see the fish again for a while, just felt its pulses bending along my arced rod, its surges bouncing the muscles of my forearms. I managed to slide it through the gap between rocks. The fish took line off my reel twice more, and then there was a long holding session, and then it was as if it had decided to come in.

The trout glided near my feet in the shallows. It was a brown, its nose hooked and its red spots glowing. When I released it, just at the moment when I ceased to hold it and it became wholly part of the stream again, I was washed by the surety that it would be the last fish I would see from this stretch of river until after a long, windy winter covered the stream with ice, held it white and silent and still.

So I stood and watched the water where the fish slipped from the shallows to depths, and then looked up to find a full awareness of twilight. A flight of mallards lifted from the dark background of a ridge to become suddenly visible against the sky. I knew I would have this to walk back through.

Because it was that time of evening when anything seems possible, I tried something new with Juice. We walked along the trail and every now and then I would say, "Juice, sit." It was the first time I had tried this without a leash. Walking back through the meadow grass, when I said, "Juice . . . ," his little black nose tipped up, and when I said "sit," his rear feet shuffled and his hips sank. It was in its way more thrilling than knowing I had caught such a nice fish to end my season here.

As I walked through the meadow, watching the land release itself to night, I couldn't convince myself that the *next* day wouldn't be the last warm day of autumn, that I wouldn't go out to the river and catch the four fattest browns of the year on dries the very next evening. Or the one after that.

Fifteen years later, Juice sometimes comes when I wave for him, but I'm almost daily given the opportunity to realize how irresponsibly optimistic I once was in my beliefs about dogs and how training them happens.

When my brother was still alive, my family bought the home I now live in as a place to gather in the summer. My brother, Chris, lived in Phoenix, and my sister in Colorado, while my parents maintained the old house near Sandusky Bay in Ohio. Here in Montana, we bought a place in the country, far up a dirt road, a house surrounded by pasture, with a pond where geese raise their goslings, a meadow where foxes den, and a small creek flowing through a gallery of cottonwoods. Soon after we bought the place, my brother came to stay here. He was very sick even by then, but he wanted to oversee the remodeling of the house, and when the job was finished, he wanted just to be here for a while, to live in this place.

Chris and I fell into an easy routine that summer. I would do odd jobs—there was always a fence to fix, or weeds to pull, bare dirt to seed, reconstruction mess to clean up. Chris would execute some brain work, figuring out what the next step was and what we'd need for the next task, or he'd drive to town to pick up supplies. But every afternoon, just as the peak of the day's heat started sliding away, we would stop whatever we were doing and walk the quarter mile to the creek with our small troupe of dogs, which by then numbered three. In terms of physical exertion, the walk to the creek was about as much as Chris could handle.

When we reached the cobbled banks, he used a tall walking stick to help with his balance. We had found an elbow in the stream, a back eddy, and we would strip off our shirts and sit down there, the pool coming up to our chests. We would sit slowly, feeling the cool water wash the heat of the day's work from our skin. My Labs would crash around the stream, chasing sticks, and Chris's Sheltie would run the shallows along the bank, letting them know in sharp, jabbing barks, just how much better he could retrieve the sticks, if only he felt like getting his coat wet.

After our dip, we would walk back across the field to the house. The sun evaporated water from our shoulders, leaving a clean, tight sensation and the smell of aquatic insects on our skin. At the house Chris, who had once spent a year in Paris training for a life he imagined as a chef, would start conjuring dinner, and I would grab my seven-foot 3-weight and head back to the creek to fish a little.

Our creek is not a productive fishery. The thoughtless, greedy forestry imposed upon this valley over the years has silted in much of the stream's vital microhabitat. Irrigation drawdowns, cows trampling the channel, and the hacking away of streamside vegetation to improve homesite views leaves the water too warm in summer. A history of mining in the tributaries and high on the main stem continues to leach heavy metals and sediment into the flow. Our off-the-grid neighbors up the hill poach with worms, ten-gallon buckets, and withering efficiency. But there are times and spots, little pockets of cool, deep water, divots in the current taken by downed cottonwood trunks, where fish linger. And trout do keep trying to migrate from the Clark Fork, periodically slipping through a gamut of mergansers, herons, ospreys, and fishhooks to occupy these little niches. In other words, you never know.

On our creek, there is no better time to fish than what remains of the day after the sun has set and direct light is lost, when birds of prey lose the luminosity of their height advantage. Caddis pop like popcorn on the surface, and small mayflies float mote-like in the air. I fished a couple places on my absentee neighbor's property where a cottonwood trunk spans the entire stream, backing up water in front of its root ball and scooping out a deep oblong of pool behind it. I could catch one or two fish, maybe three. Mostly these were small trout, six- or eight-inchers painted with parr spots, and then sometimes I would hook one that went twelve or fourteen. Once I caught a nineteen-inch rainbow just near the log, but not the summer Chris lived with me.

That summer I cast over the water that was sliding toward the same color as the sky, and watched the day fall away and felt again like this was my home now. What was left of the night was only a walk back through the field, then the peaceful sharing of a meal my brother had cooked, some easy conversation, and sleep with the windows wide open. When I finished fishing, walking back from the creek in that

time suspended between day and night I could believe anything about the world and what might happen next. I could
look across the field at the lit windows in the house and believe that my brother might be moving through those yellow
boxes of light for many years to come, that this might be
what our life would be like. And this allowed me to believe
that what had led up to now, how we got this far, meant
something.

While I walked back toward the house, the stuttered
whoor of snipes rose like distant rockets from the darkening
streamsides. The whistle-edged *voom* of nighthawks dove
overhead. Deer stepped from the woods, cautious, then suddenly grazing. Where the sun had gone behind the bumpy
ridgeline, still a faint luminescence corroded the edges of the
coming inky blue dark. For a few more moments careful
shapes would be visible stepping to the edges of the field,
peeking from beneath the low branches of the forest, dropping from the sky. In this soft hole in the day, the gap between
light and dark seemed like an access, a place I could reach
back through and touch pieces of life strewn along the way to
here. If how we got this far mattered, I could believe, so too
might the things we didn't have with us anymore. In this
way, for a few moments, twilight let me wonder if I could walk
into the house and press the numbers on the phone. When I
heard her voice on the other end, I could ask . . . *Where you
live now, are there geese?*

By the time I reached the house it was always dark.
Through the open windows light and the sizzle of sauté
spilled into the yard, and I could usually hear my brother's
voice, enlightening the dogs in the finer points of something
like béchamel sauce. The voice drew me in, and then it was

time to sit down with Chris and eat, because time was something we were running out of. We had yet to talk about everything that mattered. We had yet to cobble together all the
moments I might believe I could touch in some future day's
wonder time.

About the Author

Jeff Hull has written for *The Atlantic Monthly, Audubon, National Geographic Traveler, Outside, Travel & Leisure, National Geographic Adventure, Outdoor Life, Fortune, Men's Journal, Fly Rod & Reel, Fly Fisherman, American Angler*, and more. He has guided in Montana and remote bonefish flats in the South Pacific. He lives in Montana with his wife, Ronni, and teaches magazine writing at the University of Montana School of Journalism.